Maneuvers with Nickels and Numbers

Student Lab Book

David A. Page
Philip Wagreich
Kathryn Chval

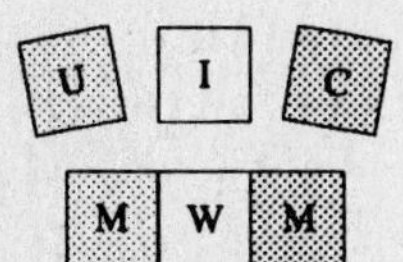

**The University of Illinois at Chicago
Maneuvers with Mathematics Project**

DALE SEYMOUR PUBLICATIONS

Other UIC-MWM Student Lab Books
Maneuvers with Rectangles
Maneuvers with Angles
Maneuvers with Triangles

(A Teacher Sourcebook is also available
for each Student Lab Book in the series.)

The Maneuvers with Mathematics Project materials were
prepared with the support of National Science Foundation
Grant No. MDR-8850466. Any opinions, findings,
conclusions, or recommendations expressed in this
publication are those of the authors and do not necessarily
represent the views of the National Science Foundation.
These materials shall be subject to a royalty-free,
irrevocable, worldwide, nonexclusive license in the
United States Government to reproduce, perform,
translate, and otherwise use and to authorize others to use
such materials for Government purposes.

Order number DS21208
ISBN 0-86651-643-3

2 3 4 5 6 7 8 9 10-MA-96 95 94

Contents

1. How Tall Is a $1,000 Stack? 1

2. How Many Nickels Can You Carry? 15

3. Will $1,000 Cover a Basketball Court? 25

4. How Much Room Is in That Box? 43

5. How Many Nickels Fit in That Box? 59

6. How Much Wrapping Paper Do I Need? 71

7. How Many Faces Do You Count? 87

8. How Big Is It? 105

**Essential contributions to
UIC-MWM were made by:**

Janice Banasiak
Corinna Ethington
Marty Gartzman
Olga Granat-Gonzalez
Andrew Isaacs
Michael Jankowski
Marlynne Nishimura
Mary Jo Porn
Aimee W. Strawn
Mahalia Triplett

Production Assistants:

Lauren Dolber
Kimberly Hanus
Tanya Henderson
Karen Herzenberg
Tracy Ho
Alex Mak
Stacie McCloud
Erik Merkau
Jennifer Lynná Mundt

Artist:

Lisa Fucarino

**The University of Illinois Maneuvers with
Mathematics Project (UIC-MWM) started
in July, 1989 under the direction of
David A. Page and Philip Wagreich of UIC.
Earlier versions were pilot tested in the
following schools in the city of Chicago:**

Boone Elementary School
Copernicus Elementary School
Jungman Elementary School
Ray Elementary School

and in these Chicago suburban schools:

Central Junior High School, Tinley Park
East Prairie School, Skokie
Finley Junior High School, Chicago Ridge
Hillel Torah Day School, Skokie
Humphrey Middle School, Bolingbrook
St. Germaine School, Oak Lawn
Transfiguration School, Wauconda
Worth Junior High School, Worth

1. How Tall Is a $1,000 Stack?

Every year, Polygon School holds a fair to raise money for the eighth grade trip. This year, the students set up over one hundred booths, including basketball contests, video arcades, candy sales, and many games.

The final event at the fair was a nickel stacking contest. Teams of students tried to stack the most nickels. The winning team stacked 53 nickels.

1. Predict how many nickels you could stack before they fall.

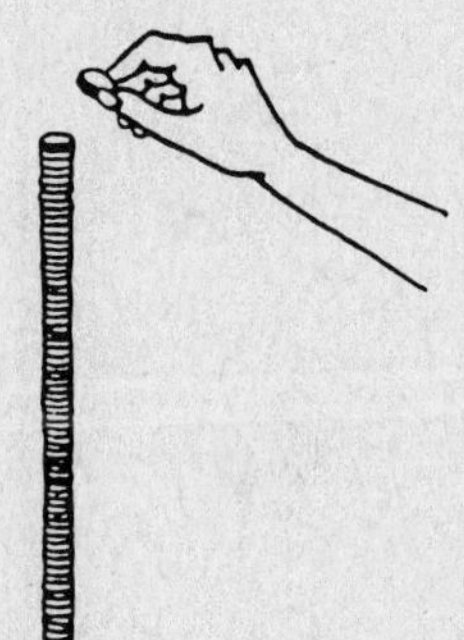

Prediction _________________

2. How many nickels can you stack? Try it.

Number of nickels _________________

The next day, the Fair Committee counted the coins they earned. Since many of the booths charged 5¢ or 15¢, most of the coins were nickels. The eighth graders were excited that they raised $1,000 worth of nickels.

3. You know it is impossible to stack $1,000 worth of nickels. However, imagine a stack of $1,000 worth of nickels. How high do you think the stack would reach? Place a check mark next to your prediction.

   _______ The doorknob

   _______ A basketball player's height

   _______ The ceiling

   _______ The school building

   _______ A 10-story city building

   _______ The Sears Tower

4. How would you figure out the height of a $1,000 stack of nickels?

Mrs. Jordan asks her class to find the height of $1,000 worth of nickels. The students decide to first figure out how many nickels are in $1,000.

5. Complete the following table to find the number of nickels in $1,000. The picture next to Problem 5b means solve the problems in your head.

		Value	Number of Nickels
	5a.	$0.10	2
	5b.	$0.50	
	5c.	$1.00	
	5d.	$2.40	
	5e.	$10.00	
	5f.		210
	5g.		1,240
	5h.	$100.00	
	5j.	$140.75	
	5k.		10,000
	5m.	$1,000.00	

Now that the students in Mrs. Jordan's class know how many nickels are in $1,000, they measure the thickness of one nickel to calculate the height of a $1,000 stack.

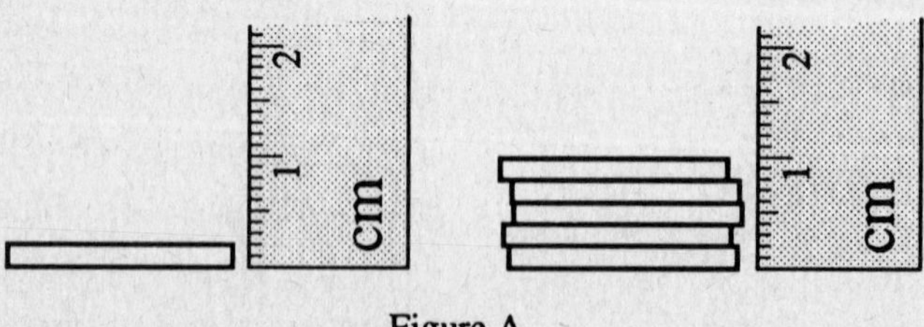

Figure A

6. Marta, a student, says, "It would be better to measure a stack of nickels to find the thickness of one nickel."

Do you agree with Marta? ________________

Yes or No

Why or why not? ____

7a. Build a stack of nickels and measure it in millimeters (mm).

7b. Draw a sketch of your stack at the right.
Label the height of the stack and the
number of nickels in the stack.

8a. Now find the thickness of *one* nickel.

Thickness of one nickel _________________ mm
Round to the nearest hundredth.

8b. List your keystrokes for Problem 8a.

☐ ☐ ☐ ☐

9. Record your data and your classmates' data in the following table.

Class Measurements			
Student or Team	Number of Nickels Stacked	Height of Stack *Put in units.*	Thickness of One Nickel *R to the nearest hundredth.*
			mm
			mm
			mm
			mm
			mm
			mm
			mm

10. Compare the measurements for the thickness of one nickel in the table.
Why did different teams get different answers?

____

11a. As a class, agree on the thickness of one nickel using the data in the table.

Thickness of one nickel _______________ mm

11b. Explain how your class decided which thickness to use.

____

                    Maneuvers with Nickels and Numbers

12. The students in Mrs. Jordan's class have not yet recorded their data. Use the following pictures to fill in the blanks.

12a. Janice:

"The height of five nickels is one cm, so one nickel is _________ mm thick."

12b. Brad:

"It takes _________ nickels to measure _________ cm or _________ mm."

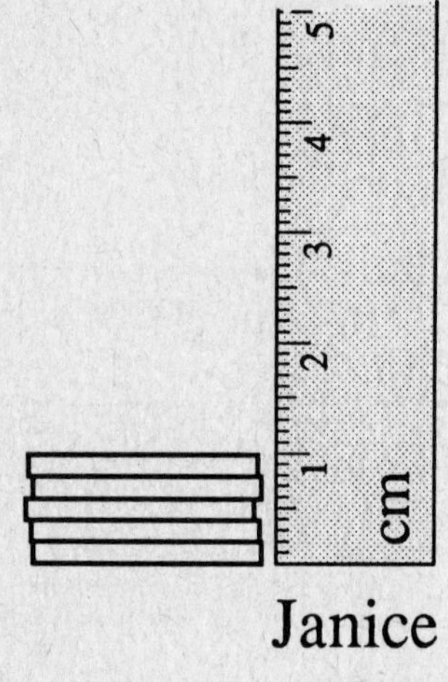

Janice

Figure B

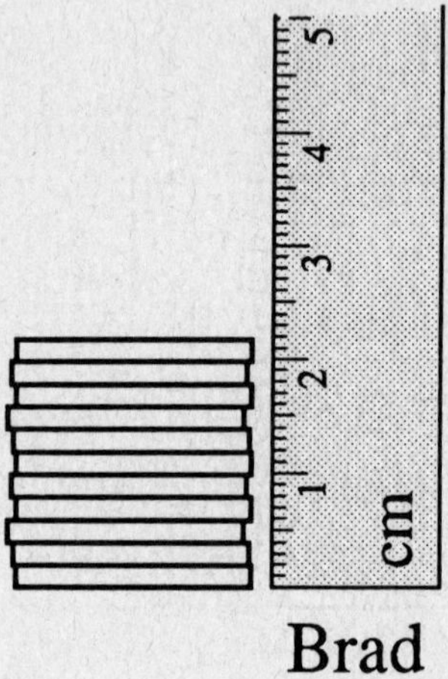

Brad

Figure C

12c. Estefan:

"A stack of _________ nickels is _________ mm high."

Sally:

"I'll stack 100 nickels and measure them." Joe replies, "You can't. It is impossible to stack 100 nickels and measure them."

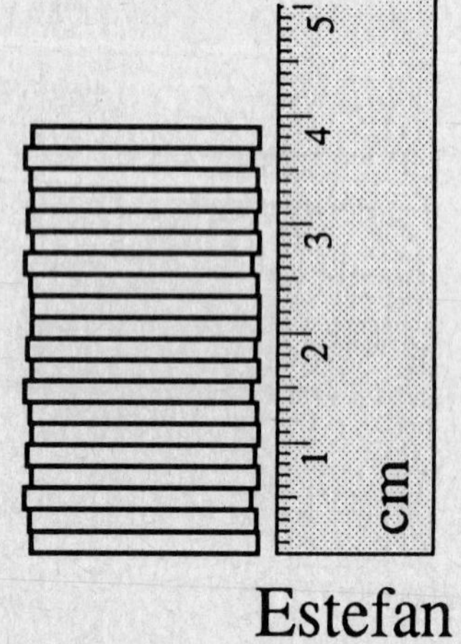

Estefan

Figure D

12d. DeMar:

"A stack of __________ nickels is __________ cm or __________ mm."

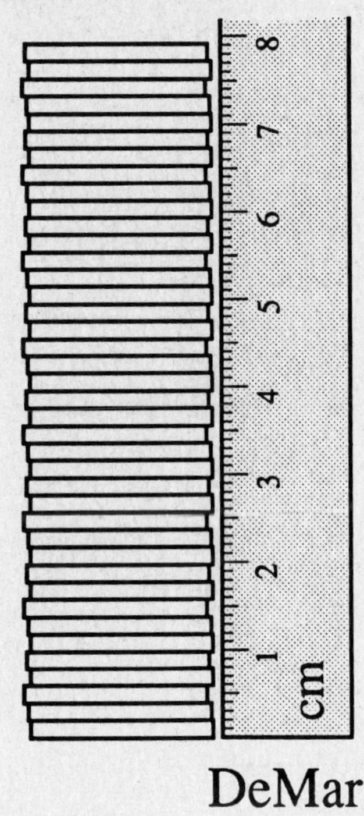

DeMar

Figure E

12e. Chad:

"A stack of ___14___ nickels is __________ cm or ___26___ mm."

Chad

Figure F

12f. Sarah:

" A whole roll of nickels measures __________ cm or __________ mm."
What should Sarah do to get a more accurate measurement?

____

____

____

____

____

Sarah

Figure G

13. Use the students' measurements on pages 4 and 5 to complete the
    following table.

Student	Number of Nickels	Height of Stack	Thickness of One Nickel *R to the nearest hundredth.*
Janice		mm	mm
Brad		mm	mm
Estefan		mm	mm
DeMar		mm	mm
Chad		mm	mm

14a. Look back at the students' rulers on pages 4 and 5. Which student,
     listed in the table above, measured *incorrectly*?

     Answer ________________

14b. What was the mistake? ____

14c. Correct this student's data in the table.

15a. As a class, determine the thickness of one nickel using the table above.

     Thickness of one nickel ________________ mm

15b. Is this thickness close to your measurement in Problem 11a? ____________

     Yes or No

16. Use the following steps to calculate the height of $1,000 worth of nickels.

16a. Number of nickels in $1,000 ________________

16b. Thickness of one nickel ________________ mm

     *Copy answer from
     Problem 11a or 15a.*

16c. Height of $1,000 stack ________________ mm

16d. It is easier to use meters when you have a large number of millimeters.
     Change the height of this stack to meters. 1,000 millimeters = 1 meter

     Height of $1,000 stack ________________ mm = ________________ m

     *Copy answer from
     Problem 16c.*

17. The following graph shows six estimated heights. Use the graph to fill in the blanks below.

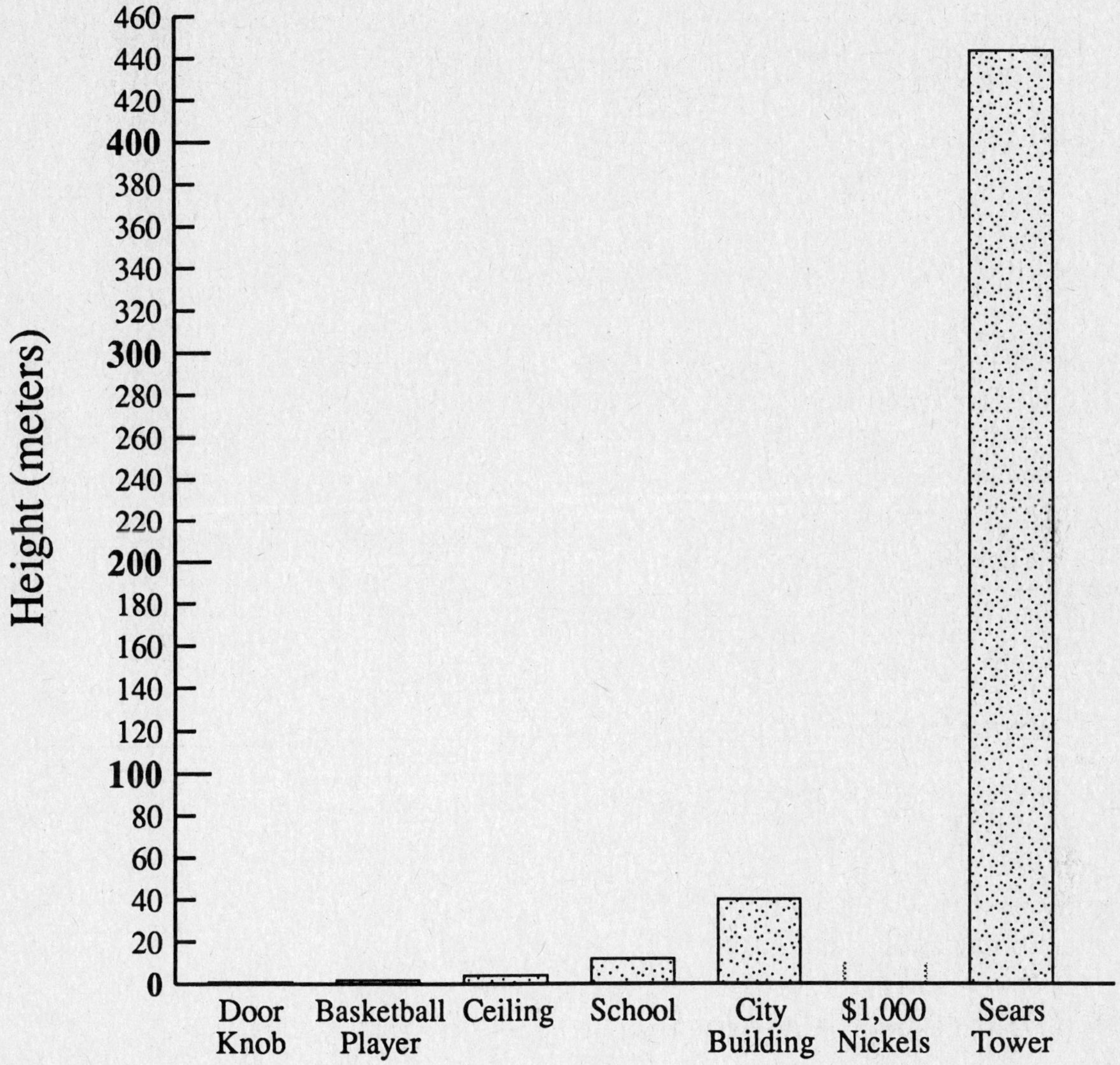

17a. The height of a basketball player is about _________ meters.

17b. The ceiling is about _________ meters high.

17c. The school building is about _________ meters.

17d. A 10-story city building is about _________ meters.

17e. The world's tallest building, the Sears Tower, is about _________ meters.

18. On the graph, make a bar for the $1,000 stack of nickels.

19. What object in the graph is close in height to the $1,000 stack of nickels.

Answer _______________

Try It Out!

1. Predict the height of $1,000 stacks by answering the following questions. Circle the stack that you predict is *taller.* Explain your thinking.

1a. $1,000 worth of nickels   or $1,000 worth of pennies

Explain. ____

1b. $1,000 worth of nickels   or $1,000 worth of dimes

Explain. ____

1c. $1,000 worth of nickels   or $1,000 worth of quarters

Explain. ____

1d. Rank these $1,000 stacks from tallest to shortest.

_______________ _______________ _______________ _______________
   Tallest   *Shortest*

2. Complete the following table.

	Coin	Thickness of Coin	Number of Coins in $1,000	Height of $1,000 Stack	Height of $1,000 Stack
2a.	Quarter	1.75 mm		mm	m
2b.	Dime	1.35 mm		mm	m
2c.	Nickel	1.98 mm	20,000	mm	m
2d.	Penny	1.57 mm		mm	m

3. Use the data in the table to rank the $1,000 stacks from tallest to shortest. Compare your calculated answers with your predictions in Problem 1d.

_______________ _______________ _______________ _______________
   Tallest   *Shortest*

4. The U.S. government's official thickness of one nickel is 1.98 mm. Is this close to your measurement in Problem 16b on page 6?

Answer _______________
    Yes or No

5a. Now that you have ranked the $1,000 stacks from tallest to shortest, make a bar for each stack. Notice the height on the graph is measured in meters.

Height of $1,000 Stacks

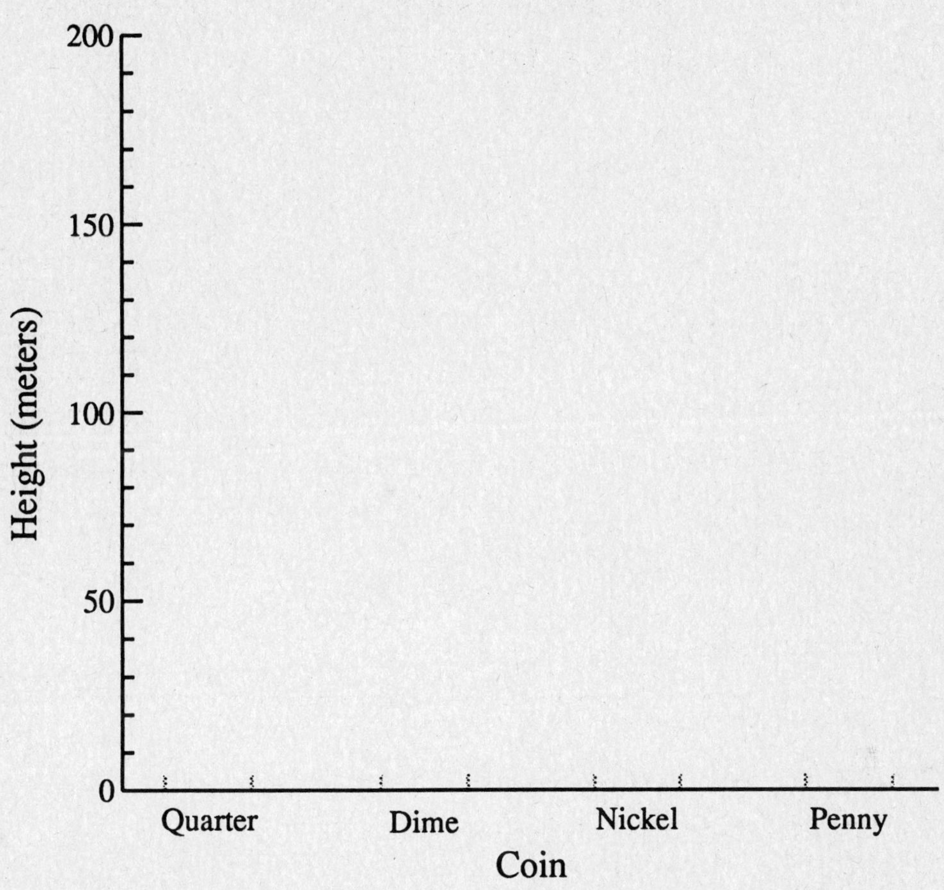

5b. Compare the height of each bar with your answers to Problem 3.

Use the table on page 8 to answer the following questions.

6. A penny is not the thickest coin, yet it forms the tallest stack. Why?

____

7a. Which coin is the thinnest? _______________

7b. Does this coin form the shortest stack? Why or why not?

____

____

____

  Maneuvers with Nickels and Numbers

Homework 1: How Tall Is a $1,000 Stack?

1. The bank provides nickels in rolls. A roll of nickels is worth $2.00.

1a. How many nickels are in one roll? ________________

1b. How many nickels are in five rolls? ________________

1c. How many nickels are in fifty rolls? ________________

2a. Look at the stack of 45 nickels at the right.
How many *full* rolls can you make with these nickels?

Number of full rolls ________________

2b. How many loose nickels will be left over?

Number of loose nickels left over ________________

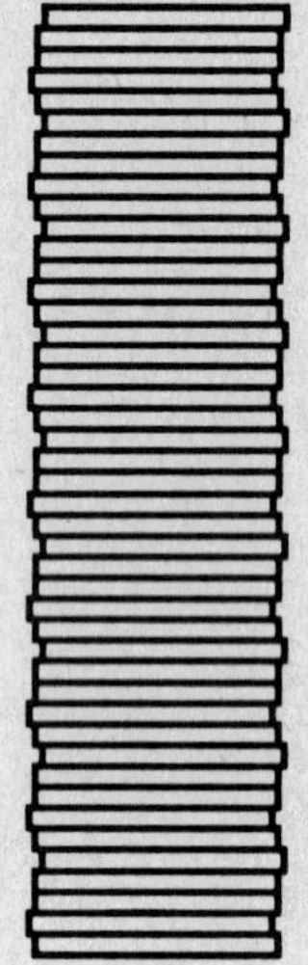

Figure H

3. Jillian has 4 rolls of nickels and 23 loose nickels.
How much money does she have?

Answer $________________

4. Complete the following table.

	Value in Dollars	Number of Nickels	Number of Full Rolls	Number of Loose Nickels Left Over
4a.	$0.30	6	0	6
4b.	$1.80	36		
4c.		80		0
4d.	$5.00			
4e.			4	7
4f.	$20.50			
4g.			149	3
4h.		8,473		
4j.	*You make one up.*			

                    © *David A. Page, Philip Wagreich*

5. A plastic checker is 4 mm high. What is the thickness of one checker in *centimeters*?

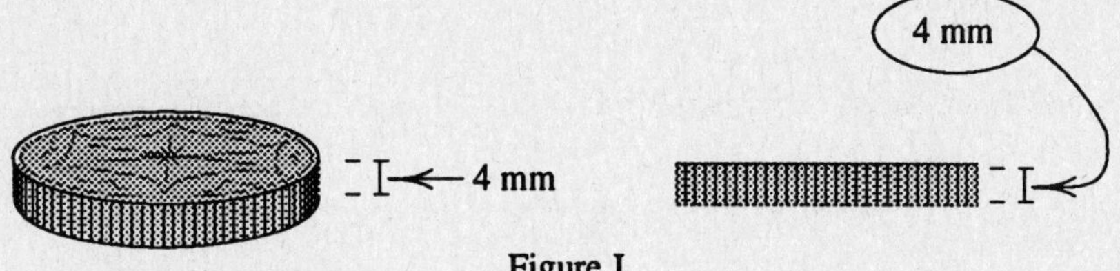

Figure J

Thickness of one checker ___________________ cm

6. How tall is a stack of ten checkers?

6a. Height of ten checkers ________________ mm

6b. Height of ten checkers ________________ cm
Notice the unit.

7. How tall is a stack of 250 checkers?

7a. Height ________________ mm

7b. Height ________________ cm
Notice the unit.

7c. Height ________________ m

8a. How tall is a stack of 221 checkers?

Height ________________ cm

8b. Tasha's answer for Problem 8a was 884 cm. How could you help Tasha?

____

9a. How many checkers does it take to reach the height of 132 cm?

______ more than 132 checkers

______ less than 132 checkers

9b. Calculate the number of checkers in this stack. Show your work.

Number of checkers ________________

10a. Ed said, "A stack of 50 checkers is 2 m high." Is he correct? _______________
Yes or No

10b. Fill in the blanks for the height of 50 checkers.

Height _______________ mm or _______________ cm or _______________ m

11. Complete the following table.

	Number of Checkers	Height of Stack (mm)	Height of Stack (cm)
11a.	500		
11b.	513		
11c.		44 mm	
11d. *Not 22.*			88 cm
11e.			164.8 cm

12. Fill in the missing units.

12a. A stack of 600 checkers is 2,400 _______.

12b. A stack of 1,500 checkers is 6,000 _______.

12c. A stack of 1,575 checkers is 630 _______.

12d. A stack of 1,755 checkers is 702 _______.

13. Fill in the blanks.

13a. A stack of _______ checkers is 3,004 mm.

13b. A stack of _______ checkers is 3,004 cm.

13c. A stack of _______ checkers is 304 mm.

14. How many checkers would equal the height of $1,000 worth of nickels?
Use your answer from Problem 2c on page 8. Show your work.

Answer _______________ checkers

* 15a. A quarter is 1.75 mm thick. Imagine a stack of quarters as tall as the Sears Tower (443 meters). Calculate the number of quarters in this stack. Show your work.

Number of quarters ______________________

R to the nearest whole number.

15b. How much is this stack of quarters worth? $______________________

16. Ask a classmate to measure your height to the nearest centimeter.

16a. Your height ________________ cm

16b. Now change your height to millimeters.

Your height ________________ mm

17. Use the following table to calculate the number of stacked coins that is equal to your height. Find the value of each stack.

	Coin	Thickness of Coin	Your Height	Number of Coins in Stack R to the nearest coin.	Value of Stack
17a.	Penny	1.57 mm	mm		$
17b.	Nickel	1.98 mm	mm		$
17c.	Dime	1.35 mm	mm		$
17d.	Quarter	1.75 mm	mm		$

18. Shafer is told his height of 1,743 mm is worth $249.00. What type of stack makes this statement true? Show your work.

Coin ______________________

19. Stack one quarter, one nickel, one penny, and one dime on top of each other. Imagine repeating this pattern until you make one large stack equal to your height. Use the steps below and the information from the table on page 13 to calculate the value of this large stack.

] One Foursome

Figure K

19a. What is the height of one foursome (1 quarter, 1 nickel, 1 penny, 1 dime)?

Answer ________________
Put in units.

19b. How many *whole* foursomes are as close as possible to your height?

Answer ________________

19c. How much is this stack worth?

Value of stack $________________

20a. Imagine stacking whole foursomes until you get as close as possible to $1,000. How many whole foursomes would you need?

Answer ________________

20b. What extra coin would you need to reach $1,000? ________________

21a. Compare the stack of foursomes in Problem 20 (it is close to $1,000) and the $1,000 stack of nickels. Predict which stack is taller.

Prediction ________________

21b. Calculate which stack is taller. Use the table on the previous page for the necessary information. Show your work.

Taller stack ________________

21c. What is the difference in height between the two stacks? ________________
Put in units.

2. How Many Nickels Can You Carry?

Polygon School has an account at the local bank. The Fair Committee asks Mrs. Jordan to deposit the $1,000 worth of nickels into the account. Patty and Bart, two students, volunteer to carry the coins to the bank.

1a. The bank is eight blocks from the school. Do you think two students from your class could carry $1,000 worth of nickels for eight blocks?

Answer _______________
Yes or No

1b. If not, predict the least number of students needed to carry the nickels.

Answer _______________

2. How could you figure out the number of students needed to carry $1,000 worth of nickels?

____

____

____

____

____

Mrs. Jordan asks her class to find the weight of $1,000 worth of nickels. Her students decide to find the weight of one nickel first.

3. Should the students weigh one nickel or several nickels? _______________
One or Several

Why? _______________________________

____

____

4a. How many nickels will you weigh? _________________

4b. Weigh your nickels in grams (g).

Weight of _________________ nickels is _________________ grams.

4c. Weight of *one* nickel _________________ grams
R to the nearest hundredth.

5a. Record your data and your classmates' data in the following table.

Class Measurements			
Student or Team	Number of Nickels Weighed	Weight of Nickels	Weight of One Nickel *R to the nearest hundredth.*
		g	g
		g	g
		g	g
		g	g
		g	g
		g	g
		g	g
		g	g
		g	g
		g	g
		g	g
		g	g
		g	g
		g	g
		g	g

5b. Teams of students in Mrs. Jordan's class collected the following data. Use this data to complete the table on page 16.

Team #1: 11 nickels seemed to weigh 55.15 g.

Team #2: 4 nickels weigh 20.5 g.

Team #3: 10 nickels weigh 49 g.

Team #4: It takes 5 nickels to weigh 25 g.

Team #6: A roll of 40 nickels weighs 201 g.

Team #5: Two nickels weigh 9.5 g.

Team #7: We found that it takes 16 nickels to weigh 79.5 g.

Team #8: We put 54 nickels into a quarter cup.
Both the nickels and the cup weighed 300 g.
The empty cup weighed about 30 g.

5c. Why is it possible to get different answers for the weight of one nickel?

____

6a. As a class, agree on the weight of one nickel.

Weight of one nickel _________________ g
R to the nearest hundredth.

6b. Explain how your class decided which weight to use.

____

7. How many nickels are in $1,000?

Answer _______________ nickels

8. Calculate the weight of $1,000 worth of nickels.

Weight of $1,000 worth of nickels _______________ g

It is easier to use kilograms when you have a large number of grams.
One thousand-something is called ***one kilo***-something.
1,000 grams (g) = ***1 kilo***gram (kg)

9. Find the weight of $1,000 worth of nickels in kilograms.

_______________ g = _______________ kg
Copy answer from Problem 8.

     Maneuvers with Nickels and Numbers

10. Since you are more familiar with pounds (lbs.), change your answer from kilograms to pounds using the following steps.

1 kilogram   =   2.2 pounds

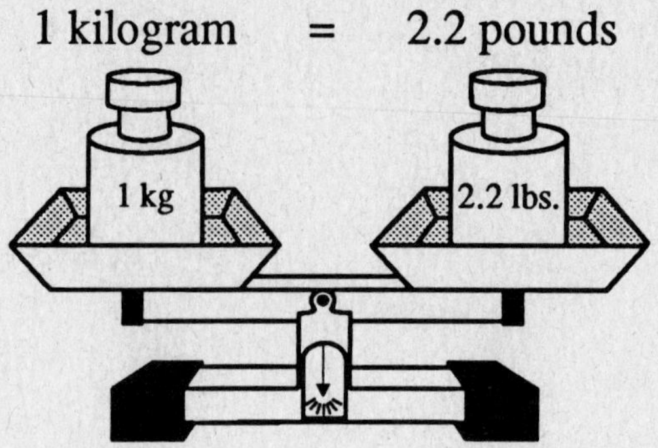

2 kilograms   =   4.4 pounds

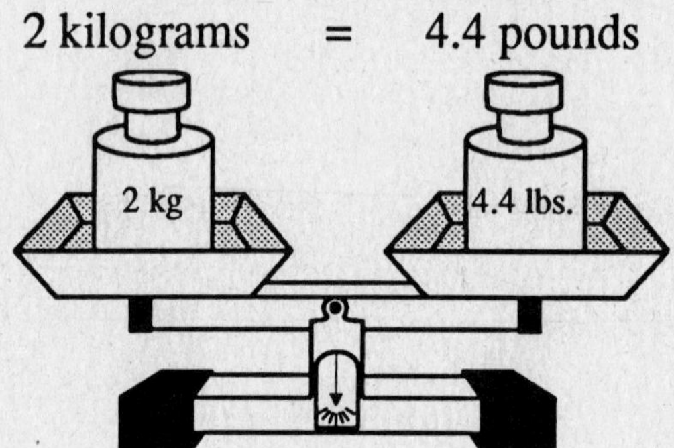

10a. How many pounds equal 10 kilograms?

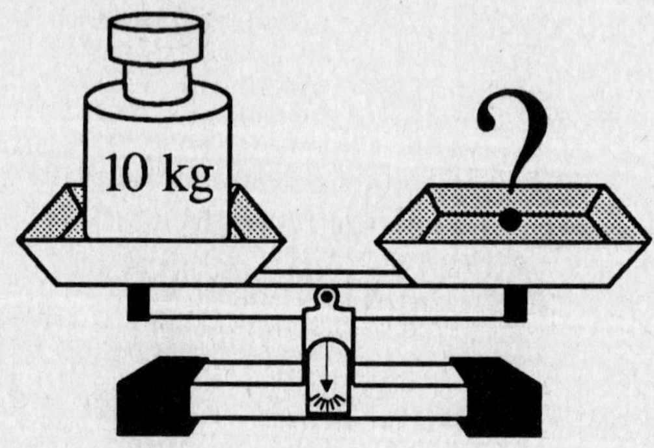

Answer _________________ lbs.

10b. How many pounds equal 100 kilograms?

Answer _________________ lbs.

10c. Use the answer from Problem 9 to find the weight of $1,000 worth of nickels in pounds.

Weight _________________ lbs.

11. Now that you know the weight of $1,000 worth of nickels, find the least number of students needed to carry them using the following steps.

11a. Find objects that weigh ten pounds. (Your gym probably has ten-pound weights.) ***Carry*** these objects around the room for a few minutes. The question is ***not***, "How heavy a load could you pick up?" but rather "What is a reasonable weight that almost everyone in your class could carry for eight blocks?"

Reasonable weight _________________ lbs.

11b. How many students are needed to go to the bank?

Number of students _________________

Compare with your prediction on page 15.

Try It Out!

1a. Draw a line from each object to its sensible weight.

Baseball	0.00036 g
Speck of dust	5 g
Dollar bill	150 g
Nickel	1 g

1b. List the objects from heaviest to lightest.

____________   ______________   ______________   ____________
Heaviest   *Lightest*

2. Circle the sensible weight for each of the following objects.
   Hint: A paper clip weighs about 1 gram.
         Your social studies textbook weighs about 1 kilogram.

2a. The ring on my finger weighs	2.6 g	2.6 kg
2b. Marci, an eighth grader, weighs	45.45 g	45.45 kg
2c. A cassette tape weighs	135 g	135 kg
2d. A big dog weighs	40 g	40 kg
2e. A VCR weighs	1,000 g	100 kg
2f. 4.84 pounds of apples weigh	2.2 g	2.2 kg

3. Find objects that weigh 1 kilogram and 1 pound. Lift them.

3a. _________________________ weighs 1 kilogram.

3b. _________________________ weighs 1 pound.

3c. Which seems to be heavier? _________________
Pound or Kilogram

4. Compare the following weights. In four of the problems, it's easy to tell which weight is heavier. Circle the heavier weight when it's "easy to tell."

4a. 1 kilogram   or   1 pound

4b. $\frac{1}{2}$ kilogram   or   1 pound

4c. 2 pounds   or   2 kilograms

4d. 1 kilogram   or   2 pounds

4e. 3 kilograms   or   1 pound

4f. 1 kilogram   or   3 pounds

5. You cannot carry $1,000 worth of nickels. Predict how many dollars worth of nickels you can carry.

Prediction $______________

6. Calculate the number of nickels you can carry using the following steps.

6a. How many pounds can you carry? ______________ lbs.

6b. Change your answer to kilograms and then to grams.

______________ lbs. = ______________ kg = ______________ g
Copy answer from Problem 6a.   *Copy window.*   *R to the nearest gram.*

6c. The official weight of one nickel is 5 grams. How many nickels can you carry? Show your work.

Answer ______________ nickels
R to the nearest nickel.

7. What is the dollar value of the nickels you can carry?

Answer $______________
Compare with Problem 5.

8. Different loads of coins are compared in the following problems. Circle the load that you predict is *heavier*. Explain why you chose your answer.

8a. $1,000 worth of nickels   or $1,000 worth of dimes

Explain. ____

8b. $1,000 worth of nickels   or $1,000 worth of pennies

Explain. ____

8c. $1,000 worth of nickels   or $1,000 worth of quarters

Explain. ____

9. Use your predictions to rank the following loads from heaviest to lightest.

$1,000 worth of quarters
$1,000 worth of dimes
$1,000 worth of nickels
$1,000 worth of pennies

______________	______________	______________	______________
Heaviest			*Lightest*

10. Using the government's official weight for each coin, calculate the weight of $1,000 worth of each coin.

Coin	Official Weight of One Coin	Number of Coins in $1.00	Official Weight of $1.00	Weight of $1,000
Quarter	5.670 g		g	g
Dime	2.268 g		g	g
Nickel	5.000 g		g	g
Penny	2.500 g		g	g

11. Officially, there is a "tie." Which two loads weigh the same?

Answer ___________________ and ___________________

12. Use Problem 10 to rank the loads again from heaviest to lightest. Compare your answers with your predictions above.

______________	______________	______________	______________
Heaviest			*Lightest*

    Maneuvers with Nickels and Numbers

Homework 2: How Many Nickels Can You Carry?

1. A team of students collected the following data about Kennedy half dollars.

1. The Kennedy half dollar has been around since 1964.

2. The Kennedy half dollars minted after 1970 are lighter because they were made with less silver. Our class weighed half dollars that were minted after 1970.

3. $10 worth of half dollars weighs 227 g.

4. My mother has a special keepsake box full of half dollars that weighs 1,005 g. The empty box weighs 360 g.

5. 25 nickels and 12 half dollars weigh 261.08 g. Each nickel weighs 5 g.

6. A roll of nickels weighs 60.82 grams less than 23 half dollars. A roll of nickels weighs 200 g.

7. Mike weighed 20 half dollars. His data showed 20 half dollars weighed 230 g. His measurement was only 3.2 grams more than the official measurement.

8. Officially, a half dollar weighs the same as two quarters. One quarter weighs 5.67 g.

 1a. Only five of the above items help to find the weight of one half dollar. Complete the following table with those items that are helpful.

Item Number	Total Weight of Half Dollars	Number of Half Dollars	Weight of One Half Dollar
	g		g
	g		g
	g		g
	g		g
	g		g

1b. Determine the weight of one Kennedy half dollar using the information in the table.

Weight _______________ g

Read Problems 2 through 7. Tell if the statement is "could be" or "crazy."

2. A calculator weighs 112 g. Could be or crazy? _________________

3. A pencil weighs 7 kg. Could be or crazy? _________________

4. A large pizza weighs 16 kg. Could be or crazy? _________________

5. A full grown elephant weighs 64,000 g.

5a. What is its weight in kilograms? _________________

5b. What is its weight in pounds? _________________

5c. Could be or crazy? _________________

6. A pair of basketball shoes weighs 794 g.

6a. What is its weight in kilograms? _________________

6b. What is its weight in pounds? _________________

Copy window.

6c. Could be or crazy? _________________

7. Make up your own "could be" problem by filling in the following blanks.

7a. _________________ weighs about _________________ lbs.

7b. Weight in kilograms _________________

★ 8. Every year, Polygon School holds a contest to see who can build the
strongest bridge made out of plastic straws. In this year's contest, the
winning structure holds 70 MWM books. Polygon School doesn't have
the equipment to weigh all these books, but the students discover that one
MWM book weighs 180 paper clips. Four of these paper clips weigh
6 grams. Calculate how much weight the winning structure holds.
Show your work.

Weight _________________
Put in units.

          Maneuvers with Nickels and Numbers

9. For the past five years, the Cushing family saved all their coins to use toward a vacation. Mr. Cushing went to the bank to deposit the coins. A machine at the bank counted the coins. The machine recorded the following:

5,987 quarters; 5,003 dimes; 4,918 nickels; 25,033 pennies.

How much money did they save? Show your work.

Amount of money _________________
Put in units.

10. Mr. Cushing carried these coins to his car in several trips before he left for the bank. Use the following steps to calculate the number of trips he made to the car.

10a. Find the total weight of all the coins. Show your work.
One quarter weighs 5.670 g. One dime weighs 2.268 g.
One nickel weighs 5.000 g. One penny weighs 2.500 g.

Total weight of coins _________________
R to the nearest tenth.
Put in units.

10b. What is a reasonable weight that Mr. Cushing carried to his car?

Reasonable weight _________________
Put in units.

10c. How many trips did Mr. Cushing make to the car?

Number of trips _________________

3. Will $1,000 Cover a Basketball Court?

You calculated the height and weight of $1,000 worth of nickels. Imagine
spreading these nickels out on a flat surface to see how much area they cover.

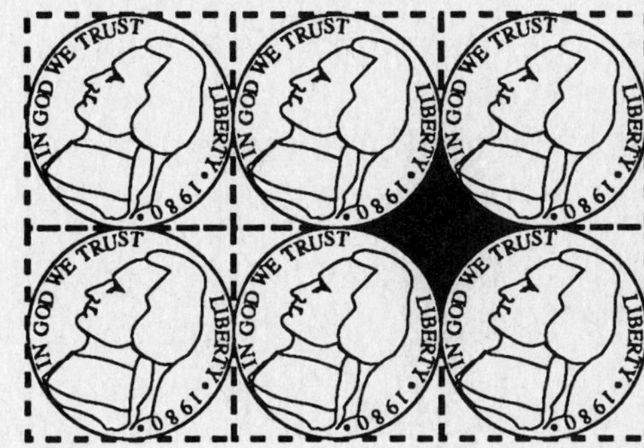

There are two ways to arrange nickels on a
flat surface. The picture at the right shows
square packing. Notice the *square* around
each nickel.

Figure A

The picture at the right shows *close
packing* (or hexagonal packing).
Notice the *hexagon* (six sides) around
each nickel.

Figure B

1. Compare the following shaded regions from Figures A and B.

Which of these shapes has less black shading? _________

A or B

There is less space between the nickels in Figure B. This means the nickels are
closer together. Close packing allows you to fit a few more nickels in an area.
However, it is easier to calculate area using square packing.

Use square packing throughout this chapter.

The distance across a circle through its center is the ***diameter.***

2. Measure the nickel's diameter to the nearest 0.1 cm.

Figure C

Nickel's diameter _________________ cm

3a. Line up ten nickels like the following *sketch.*

How many cm?

Figure D

3b. Measure the distance across the nickels to the nearest 0.1 cm.

Answer _________________ cm

3c. Use your measurement of ten nickels to find the diameter of one nickel.

Nickel's diameter _________________ cm

Should be close to Problem 2.

4. The length across seven nickels is officially 14.847 cm. Calculate the official diameter of one nickel.

14.847 cm

Figure E

Nickel's official diameter _________________ cm

5. Look back at your answers to Problems 2 and 3c. Which answer is closer to the official diameter of a nickel?

Answer _________________

Why? ____

In square packing, each nickel fits in a square. This square is called the **Home Square**. Notice that the *side* of the Home Square and the *diameter* of the nickel are the same length.

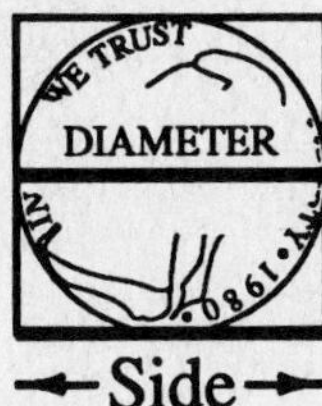

Figure F

6. The Home Square at the right is on a centimeter grid. Each centimeter square has an **area** of 1 square centimeter. Count square centimeters to estimate the area of the Home Square.

   Estimate ______________ square centimeters

Figure G

 7a. Calculate the area of the Home Square using the official diameter of a nickel.

   Press: ⬚ 2.121 ⬚ ⬚ × ⬚ ⬚ 2.121 ⬚ ⬚ = ⬚

2.121 cm

Figure H

   Area ⬚ . ⬚ 9 8 ⬚ ⬚ square centimeters

   Compare with your estimate.

Notice that you multiplied the two sides of a square to find its area. Use the *x-squared* key, ⬚ x^2 ⬚, when you multiply a number by itself. This is called *squaring a number*.

The area of the Home Square is 2.121×2.121 or 2.121^2. The little raised 2 is an *exponent*. It says: "I want to multiply two copies of 2.121."

7b. To find the area of the Home Square, press ⬚ 2.121 ⬚ ⬚ x^2 ⬚ .

   Area ⬚ . ⬚ ⬚ ⬚ 6 4 ⬚ cm^2

   Should agree with Problem 7a.

The unit cm^2 is read *square centimeters* or *centimeters squared*.

8. Count square centimeters to estimate the area of three square-packed nickels.

   Estimate ________________ cm^2

Figure J

Calculate the area of three square-packed nickels two different ways.

9. *First way:* Each nickel fits in a square.

9a. Area of Home Square __________ cm^2
      R to the nearest hundredth.

Figure K

9b. Area of three Home Squares ⬜⬜.5⬜ cm^2
      R to the nearest hundredth.

9c. Was your estimate in Problem 8 close? ________________
      Yes or No

10. *Second way:* Three nickels fit inside the rectangle at the right.

10a. Width of rectangle ____________ cm

10b. Length of rectangle ____________ cm

Figure L

10c. Multiply to find the area of the rectangle.

   Area of rectangle ____________ cm^2
      R to the nearest hundredth.
      Should agree with Problem 9b

11. Calculate the area of five square-packed nickels. Use either method.

Figure M

Area ⬜2.⬜⬜ cm^2
   R to the nearest hundredth.

12. Thirty-six nickels are square packed in the sketch at the right. Calculate the area of the rectangle.

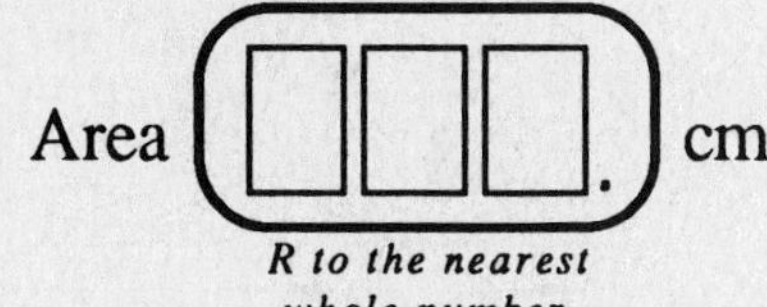

Area [ ][ ][ ] . cm^2

R to the nearest whole number.

Figure N

13. Thirty-six nickels are now packed in a different rectangle. Calculate the area of this rectangle.

Figure P

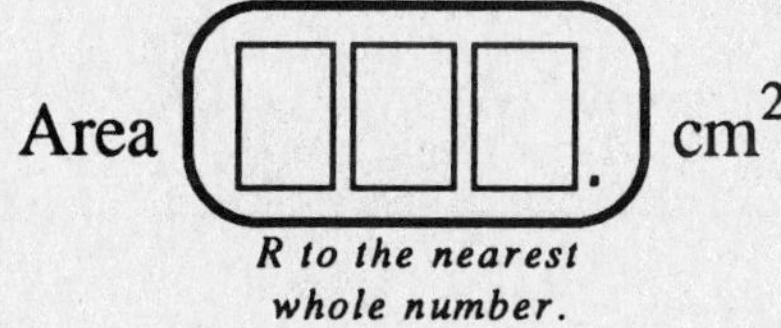

Area [ ][ ][ ] . cm^2

R to the nearest whole number.

14. Compare the areas of the rectangles in Problems 12 and 13.

    Are the answers the same? Why or why not?

    ____

15a. Draw a quick sketch showing 36 square-packed nickels inside of a *square*.

15b. Label the dimensions of the square.

15c. What is the area of this square? Show your work.

Answer ________________ cm^2

R to the nearest whole number.

          Maneuvers with Nickels and Numbers

16. Four nickels are square packed in a square. Find the side length and area of the square.

16a. Side length ________________ cm

16b. Area ________________ cm^2

R to the nearest tenth.

Figure Q

17. Nine nickels are packed in a square. Find the side length and area of the square.

17a. Side length ________________ cm

17b. Area ________________ cm^2

R to the nearest tenth.

Figure R

18. In the following problems, nickels are packed in squares. Find the area of each square. *Use 4.50 cm^2 for the area of the Home Square in the rest of this chapter.*

	Number of Nickels	Area of Square
18a.	1	4.50 cm^2
18b.	16	cm^2
18c.	81	cm^2
18d.	225	cm^2
18e.	400	cm^2

In Problem 17 on page 30, you used the side length of a square to find its area. Now you will use the area of a square to find the side length.

For example, the area of the square in Figure S is 30.25 cm^2. Korin wants to find the side length. Through trial and error, she finds that the square's side length is 5.5 cm.

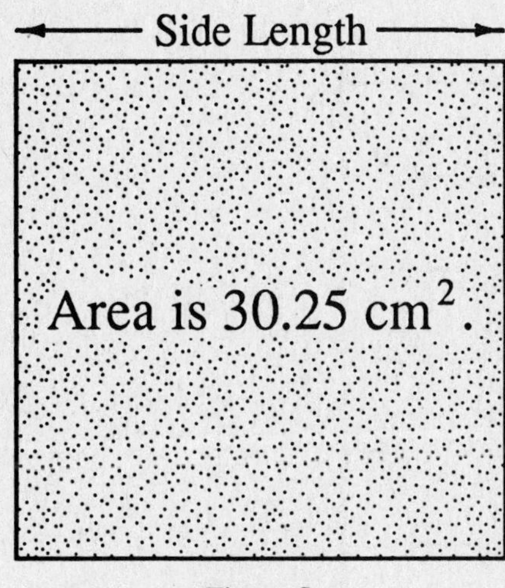

Figure S

Side Length	Area *You want 30.25 cm^2.*
5 cm	25 cm^2 *Too small.*
7 cm	49 cm^2 *Too big.*
6 cm	36 cm^2 *Too big.*
5.5 cm	30.25 cm^2 *Just right.*

Since $\boxed{5.5}\ \boxed{x^2} = 30.25$, the side length of the square is 5.5 cm.

 19. The square below is a sketch. Find the side length of the square using $\boxed{x^2}$. Label the square's side length after you complete the table.

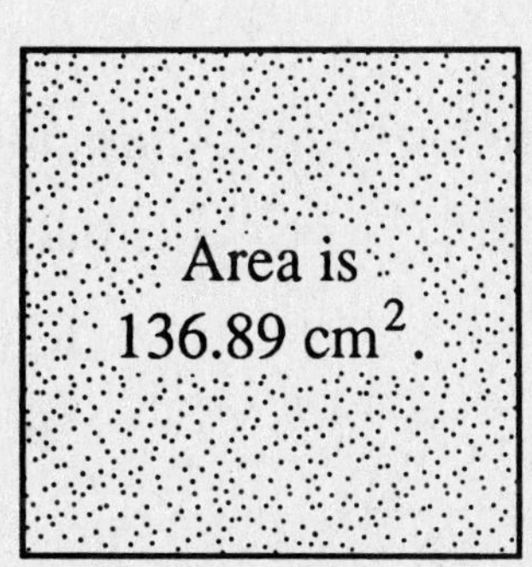

Figure T

	Side Length	Area *You want 136.89 cm^2.*
19a.	11 cm	121 cm^2 *Too small.*
19b.	12 cm	144 cm^2 *Too big.*
19c.	11.6 cm	cm^2 *Too big or too small?*
19d.	11.8 cm	cm^2
19e.	cm *What's your next try?*	cm^2
19f.	cm *What's your next try?*	cm^2
19g.	cm *What's your next try?*	cm^2

 20. By trial and error, find the side length of a square whose area is $299.29\ cm^2$. Use the following table to keep track of your trials. Don't forget to fill in the missing units.

Side Length	Area *You want 299.29 cm².*

There is a faster way to find the side length of a square when you know its area. Look at $\sqrt{x}$ directly above the $\boxed{x^2}$ key on your calculator. This is called the ***square root of x***. Press $\boxed{INV}$ to change x^2 into $\sqrt{x}$. If you know the area of a ***square***, use the square root key to find its side length.

For example, the area of a square is $81\ cm^2$.
To find the side length, press: $\boxed{81}\ \boxed{INV}\ \boxed{\sqrt{x}}$.

$\sqrt{81} = 9$, since $9 \times 9 = 81$. A square with an area of $81\ cm^2$ has sides that are 9 cm long.

What number times itself equals 81? _________________

What number times itself equals 144? _________________

What number times itself equals 299.29? _________________
*Compare with
the table above.*

$\sqrt{324} =$ _________________

$\sqrt{325} =$ _________________
R to the nearest hundredth.

21. The area of the square in the sketch at the right is 156.25 cm^2. Find the side length of the square using ⌈√x⌉ key. List your keystrokes.

| 156.25 | | |

Side length _________________ cm
The answer is less than 20.

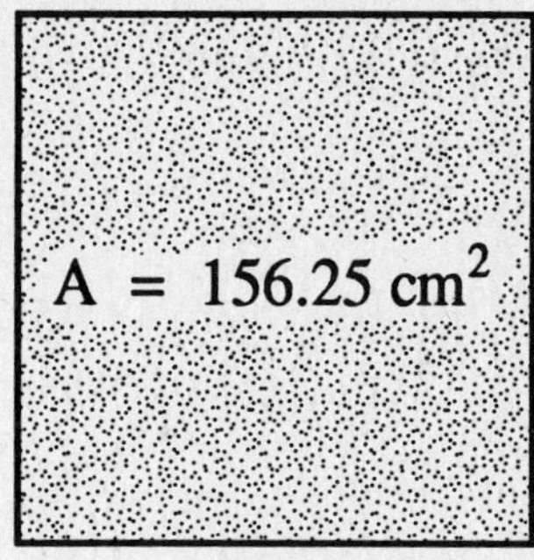

Figure U

22. The area of a square is 243.36 cm^2. Find the side length of the square.

Side length _________________ cm

23. Forty-nine nickels are packed in a square. Use ⌈√x⌉ to find the number of nickels along each side.

Answer _________________ nickels

24. Three hundred sixty-one nickels are packed in a square. Find the number of nickels along each side. List your keystrokes.

| | | |

Answer _________________ nickels

25. Complete the following table.

	Number of Nickels	Number of Nickels Along Side Length	Area of Square *R to the nearest cm^2.*	Side Length of Square *R to the nearest tenth.*
25a.	25		cm^2	10.6 cm
25b.	121		cm^2	cm
25c.	169		cm^2	cm
25d.	289		cm^2	cm
25e.	529		cm^2	cm
25f.	1,089		cm^2	cm

                Maneuvers with Nickels and Numbers

Try It Out!

1. Twelve nickels are square packed into three different rectangles in the following sketches. Calculate the area of each rectangle. Use 4.50 cm^2 as the area of one Home Square.

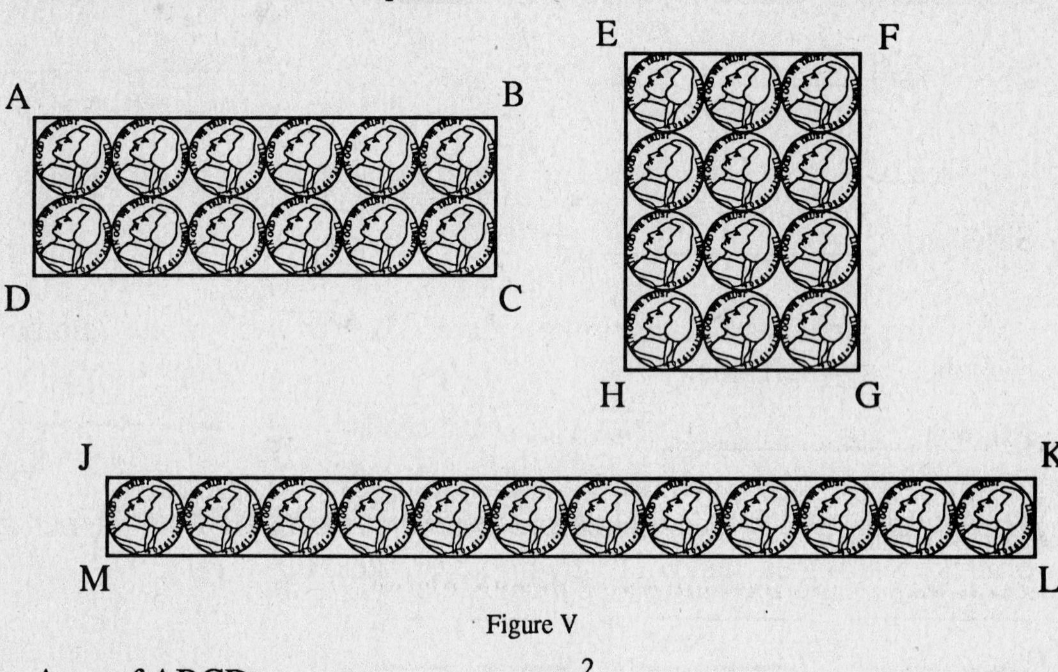

Figure V

1a. Area of ABCD _______________ cm^2

1b. Area of EFGH _______________ cm^2

1c. Area of JKLM _______________ cm^2

2a. The square at the right has an area of 54 cm^2. Do you think you could square pack 12 whole nickels in this square?

Answer _______________
Yes or No

2b. Why or why not? _______________

____

2c. Try it. Do 12 whole nickels fit in this square?

Answer _______________
Yes or No

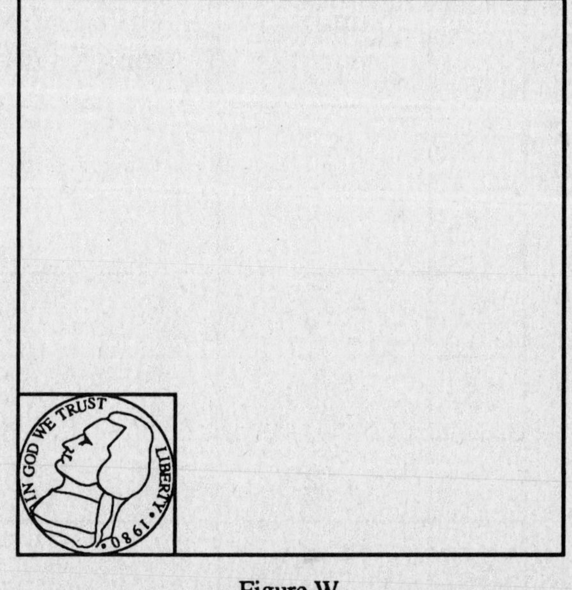

Figure W

The area of 12 Home Squares is 54 cm^2. The area of the square at the right is also 54 cm^2, but only 9 *whole* nickels fit in this square. If you put together the "extra pieces of nickels," however, the whole nickels and pieces add up to 12 nickels.

3. Estimate the number of nickels along the side length of the square at the right.

Estimate $\boxed{3}$. $\boxed{}$ nickels

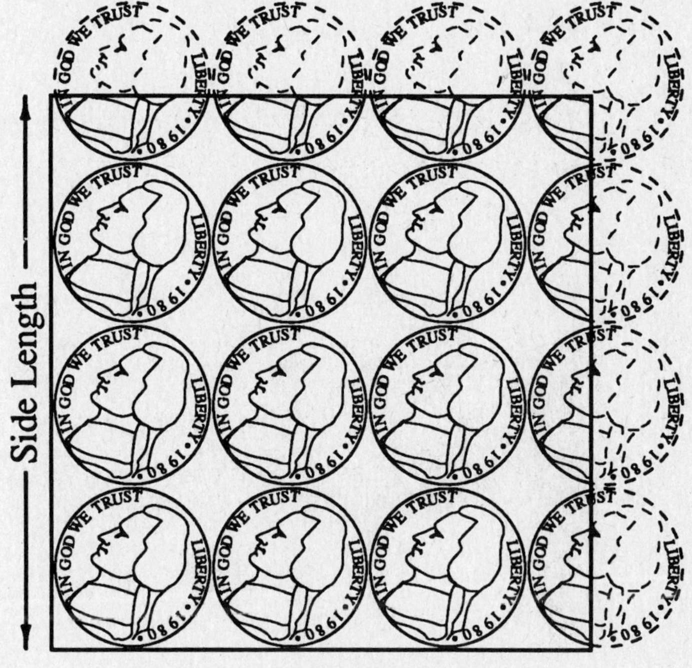

Figure X

Use the following two methods to find the side length of the square above.

4a. *First way:* Find the number of nickels that make up the side length.

Press: $\boxed{12}$ $\boxed{\text{INV}}$ $\boxed{\sqrt{x}}$

Nickels along side length ________________
R to the nearest hundredth.
Compare with Problem 3.

4b. Find the side length of the square in centimeters.

Press: $\boxed{}$ $\boxed{\times}$ $\boxed{2.121}$ $\boxed{=}$

Answer from Problem 4a.　　*Nickel's Diameter*

Side length ________________ cm
R to the nearest tenth.

5. *Second way:* Twelve Home Squares make up the area of the square. Calculate the side length of the square.

Press: $\boxed{12}$ $\boxed{\times}$ $\boxed{4.5}$ $\boxed{=}$ $\boxed{\text{INV}}$ $\boxed{\sqrt{x}}$

Number of Nickels　　*Area of Home Square*

Side length ________________ cm
R to the nearest tenth.
Should agree with Problem 4b.

　　　　Maneuvers with Nickels and Numbers

Try It Out Again!

1a. What is the dollar value of the nickels on the following table?

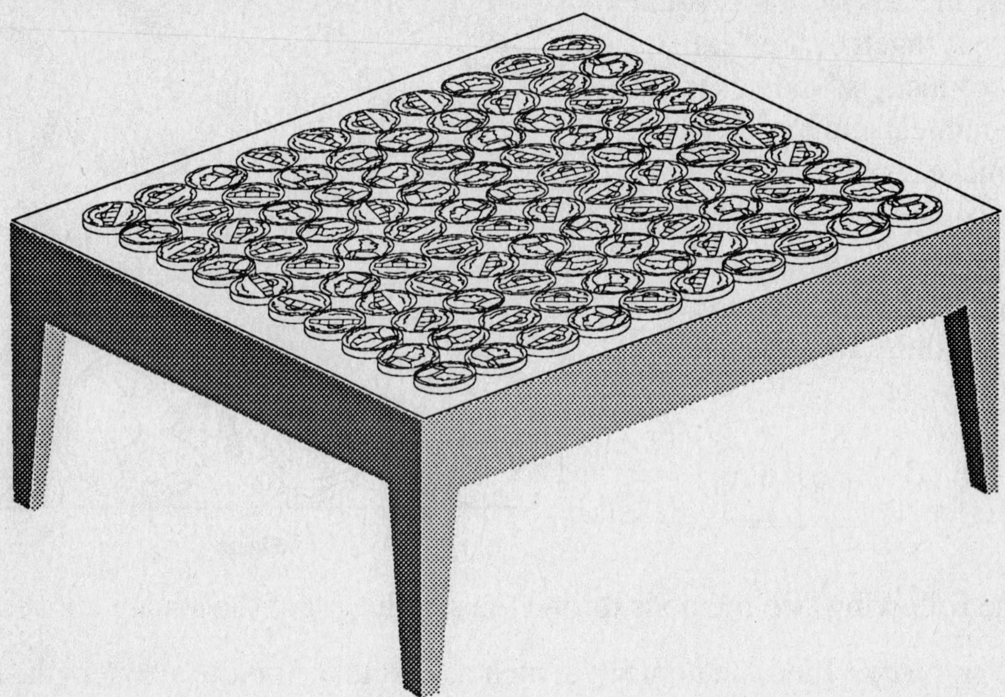

Figure Y

Answer $________________

1b. Calculate the area of the nickels on the table.

Area ________________ cm^2

1c. Calculate the side length of the square built from the nickels.

Side length ________________ cm
R to the nearest tenth.

2. Do you think the tabletop above is smaller or larger than your desktop?

Answer ________________
Smaller or Larger

3. Measure the width and length of your desktop.

3a. Width ________________ cm

3b. Length ________________ cm

4. What is the area of your desktop? ________________
Put in units.

5a. Calculate the number of square-packed nickels that fit on your desktop. Show your work.

Number of nickels _________________

5b. What is the dollar value of these nickels?

Answer $_________________

6. Suppose you square packed $1,000 worth of nickels. What is the smallest area needed to square pack them?

Check your best guess:

_________ Your desktop

_________ Your teacher's desktop

_________ The floor in your classroom

_________ A basketball court

_________ A football field

7. Calculate the area covered by $1,000 worth of nickels using the following steps.

7a. Number of nickels in $1,000 _________________

7b. Area of $1,000 worth of nickels _________________
Put in units.

8. You know the area of $1,000 worth of nickels. Calculate the side length of the *square* that has this same area.

8a. Side length _________________ cm

8b. Side length _________________ m

8c. Would a square this size fit in your classroom? _________
Yes or No

8d. Was your prediction in Problem 6 close? _________
Yes or No

     Maneuvers with Nickels and Numbers

Let's see how many nickels it would take to cover your classroom floor.
Brian, a tall eighth grader, took giant steps across his classroom to estimate the
length of the room. Each giant step was about one meter (100 centimeters)
long.

9. Estimate the size of your classroom in centimeters using Brian's method.

9a. Length of classroom _________________ cm

9b. Width of classroom _________________ cm

9c. Area of classroom _________________ cm^2

10. Calculate the number of nickels that can be square packed on your
classroom floor. Show your work.

Answer _________________ nickels
R to the nearest nickel.

11. What is the dollar value for all of these nickels? Show your work.

Answer $_________________

Homework 3: Will $1,000 Cover a Basketball Court?

 **1a.** Estimate how many square-packed nickels fit in the following rectangle.

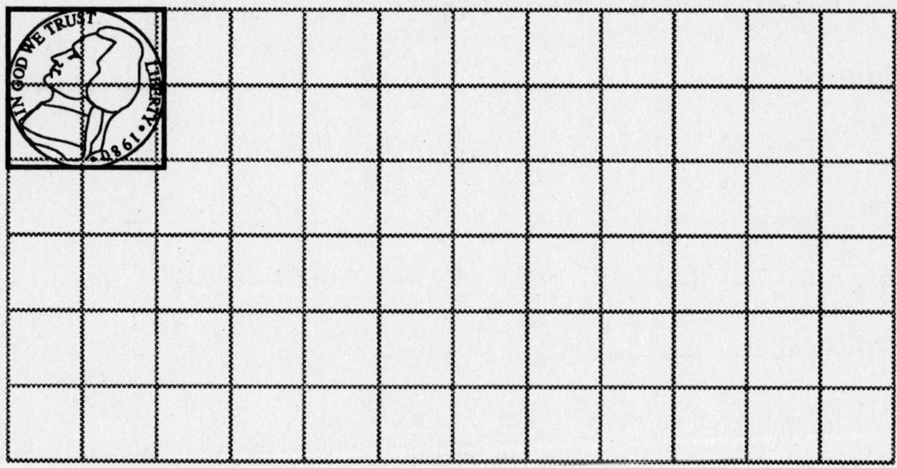

Figure Z

Estimate _______________ nickels

 **1b.** Calculate the number of square-packed nickels that fit in the rectangle in Figure Z. Show your work.

Answer _______________ nickels

 **2a.** Estimate how many square-packed nickels fit in the rectangle at the right.

Estimate _______ nickels

2b. Calculate the number of square-packed nickels that fit in the rectangle in Figure AA.

Answer _______ nickels

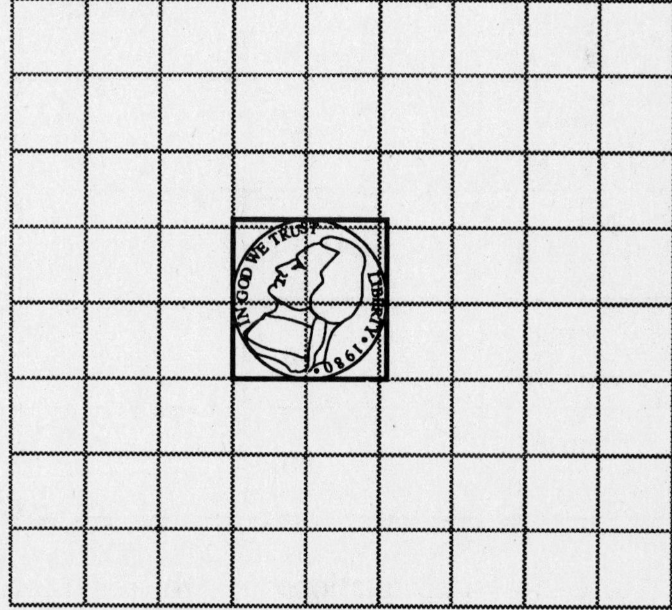

Figure AA

3. What is the same about the rectangles above?

____

4. The area of squares built from different coins are compared in the following problems. Circle the square that you predict is *larger*. Then explain why you chose your answer.

4a. $1,000 worth of pennies   or $1,000 worth of nickels

Explain. ____

4b. $1,000 worth of dimes   or $1,000 worth of nickels

Explain. ____

4c. $1,000 worth of quarters   or $1,000 worth of dimes

Explain. ____

4d. $1,000 worth of each coin is square packed into four squares. Use your predictions to rank the squares from largest to smallest.

______________   ______________   ______________   ______________
  Largest Square   *Smallest Square*

5. Calculate the side length of the squares needed to square pack $1,000 worth of each coin. Complete the following table.

Coin & Its Diameter	Area of Home Square *R to the nearest hundredth.*	Number of Coins in $1,000	Area of $1,000 Square *R to the nearest cm².*	Side Length of Square *R to the nearest cm.*
Penny 1.905 cm	cm²		cm²	cm
Nickel 2.121 cm	4.50 cm²		cm²	cm
Dime 1.791 cm	cm²		cm²	cm
Quarter 2.426 cm	cm²		cm²	cm

6. Use your calculations in Problem 5 to rank the $1,000 squares from largest to smallest.

______________   ______________   ______________   ______________
  Largest Square   *Smallest Square*

7a. $1,000 worth of square-packed pennies fits in one of the squares in the following sketch. Label that square "penny." Also label its side length.

Junior High Basketball Court

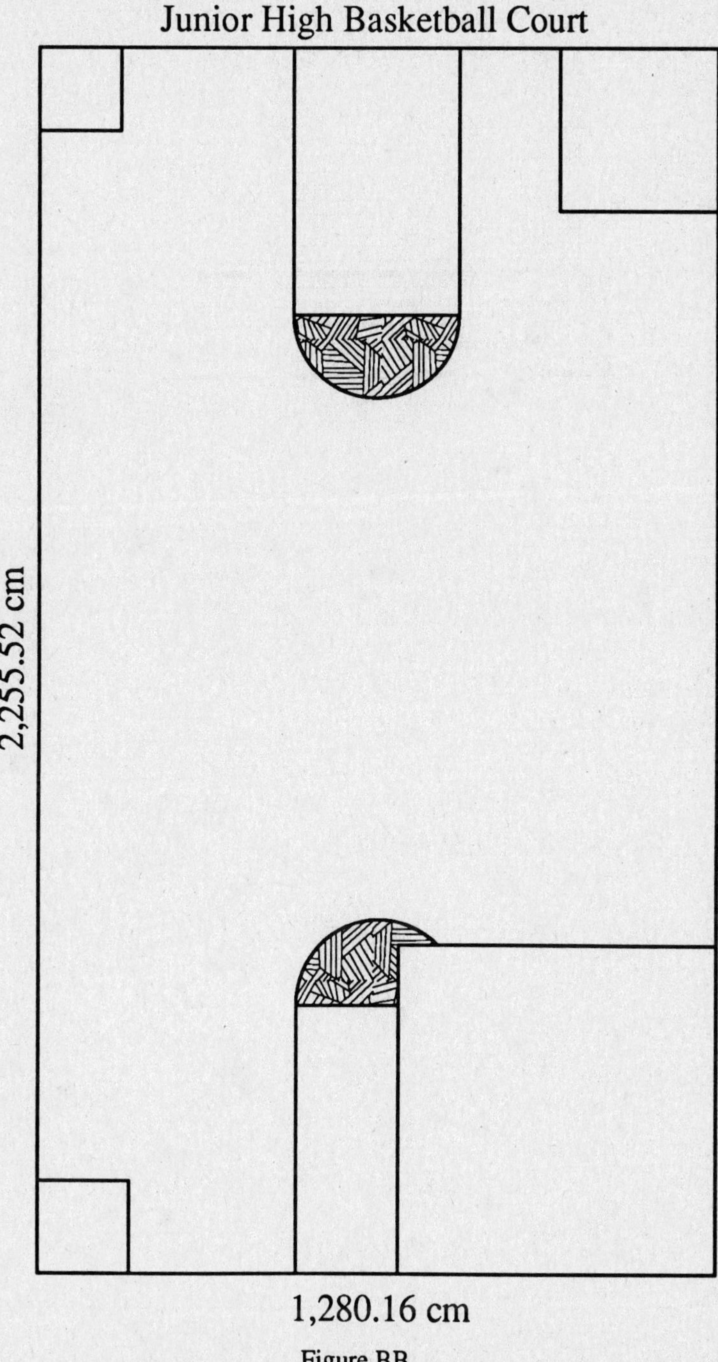

Figure BB

7b. Label the other squares "nickel," "dime," or "quarter." Also label the side length of each square.

8. Estimate how many $1,000 squares of nickels fit on this court.

Estimate _______________

9. A junior high basketball court is 1,280.16 cm (42 feet) wide and 2,255.52 cm (74 feet) long.

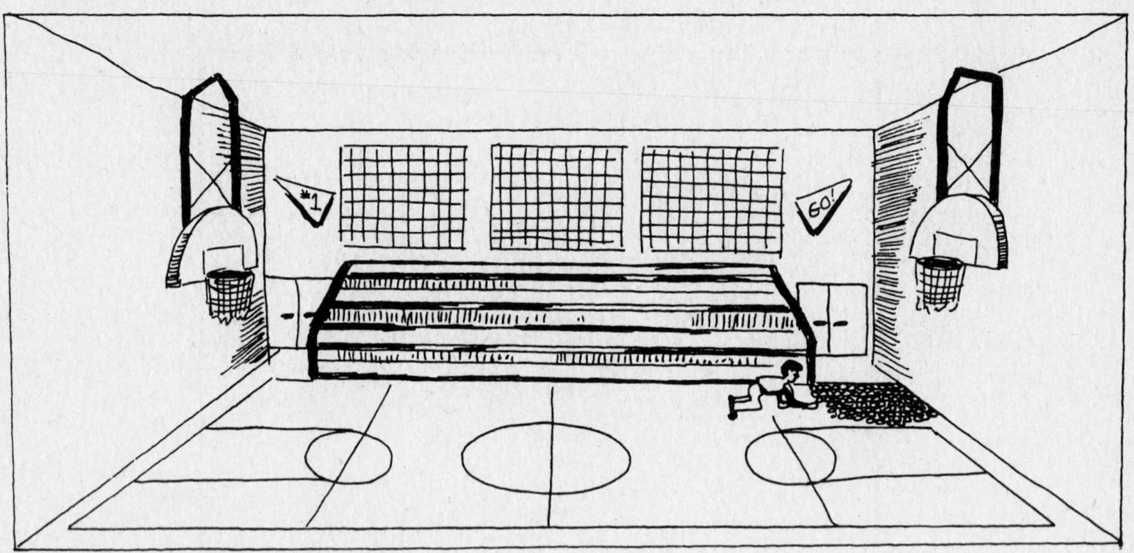

9a. Calculate the area of the basketball court.

Area _________________ cm^2

Copy window.

9b. How many nickels can be square packed on the court?

Answer _________________ nickels

R to the nearest hundred.

9c. What is the dollar value of all these nickels?

Answer $_________________

9d. Was your estimate in Problem 8 high or low? _________________

High or Low

10a. Find the dimensions of a professional basketball court in an encyclopedia or another reference book.

Dimensions _________________ by _________________

Put in units.   *Put in units.*

10b. Calculate the number of square-packed nickels that would cover this court. Show your work.

Number of nickels _________________

R to the nearest nickel.

4. How Much Room Is in That Box?

1. A *cube* is a special box. Look at the following cubes.

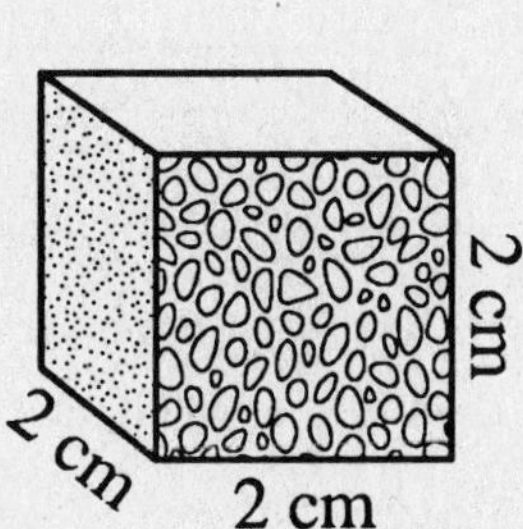

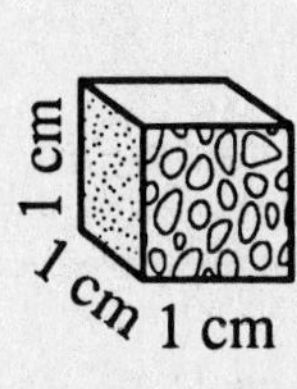

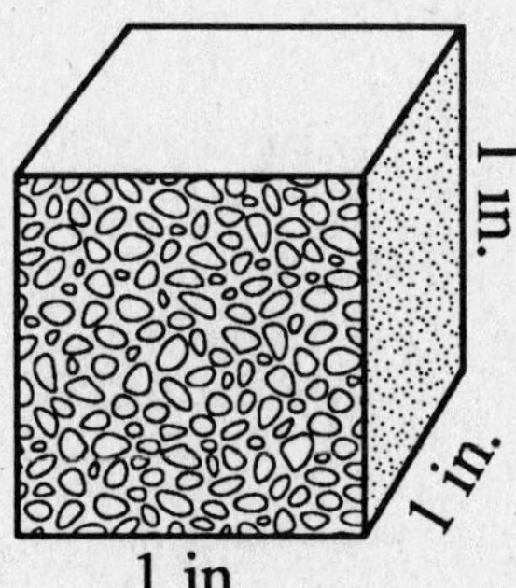

Figure A

How would you describe a cube? _______________________________

____

Here is a one-centimeter cube. It is a one-centimeter cube because its
dimensions (length, width, and height) are each 1 centimeter.
Another name for a one-centimeter cube is *centimeter cube*.

Figure B

The following figures are built from centimeter cubes. Find the number of
cubes in each figure.

2.

Figure C

Answer ____________ cubes

3.

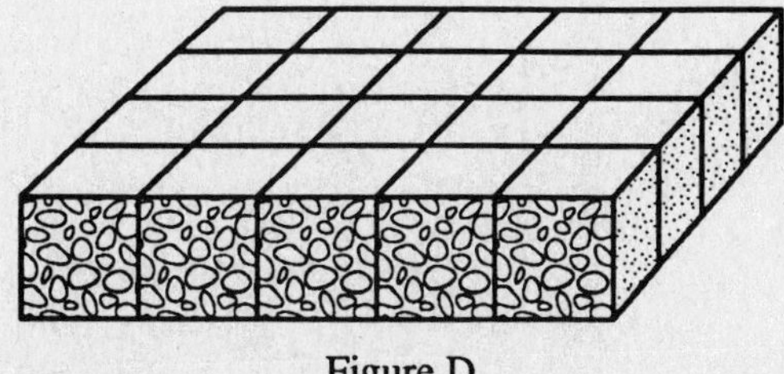

Figure D

Answer ____________ cubes

4.

Figure E

Answer ____________ cubes

The answer is not 22.

          Maneuvers with Nickels and Numbers

You can think of volume as the space in an object. Since the dimensions of the cube at the right are each 1 centimeter, the cube's volume is 1 cubic centimeter. Another way to write 1 cubic centimeter is 1 cm^3.

Figure F

5a. Five centimeter cubes are put together to form one row.

What is the volume of this row? _________ cm^3

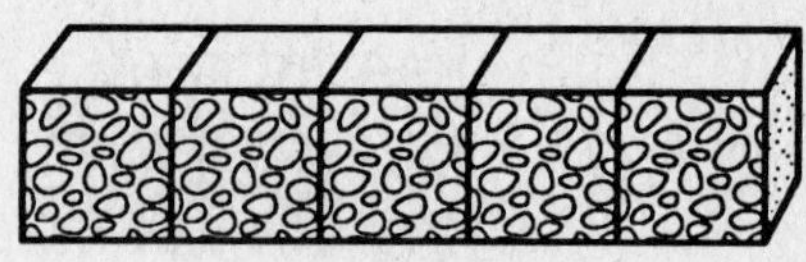
one row

Figure G

5b. Two of these rows are put together to form one layer.

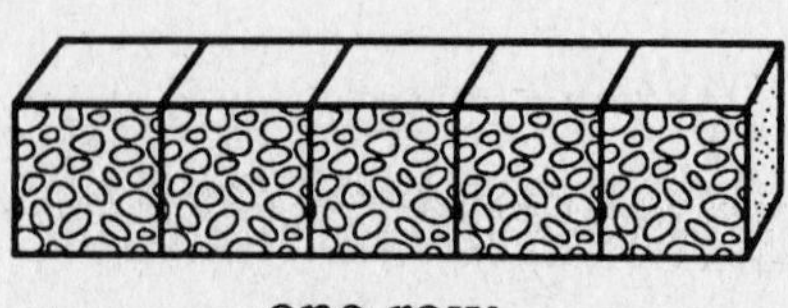
one row

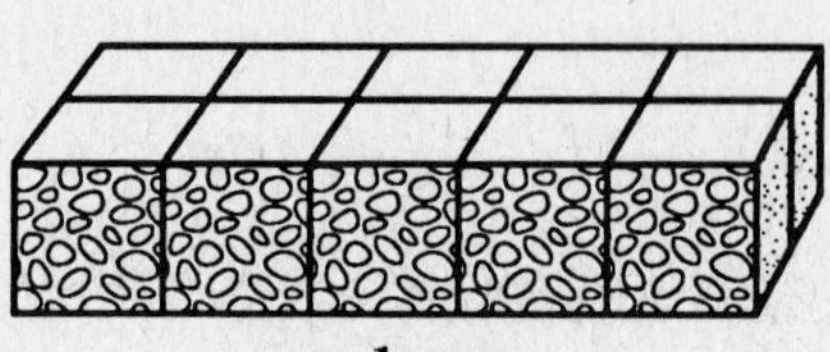
one layer

Figure H

What is the volume of this layer? _______________ cm^3

5c. Three of these layers are stacked together.

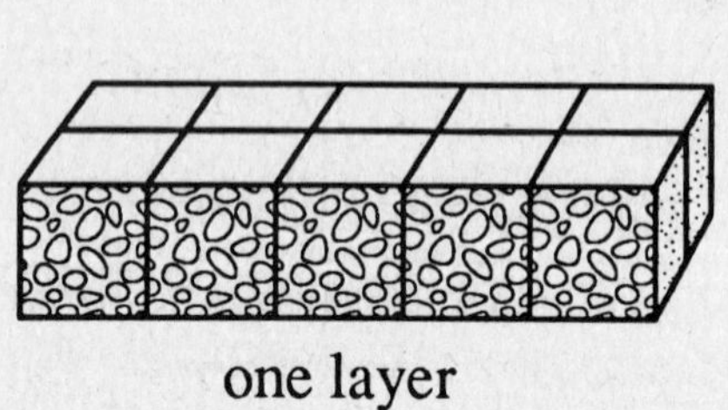
one layer

Figure J

stack

What is the volume of this stack? _______________ cm^3

5d. This stack fits perfectly inside the box at the right. What is the volume of the box?

Volume of box _______________
Put in units.

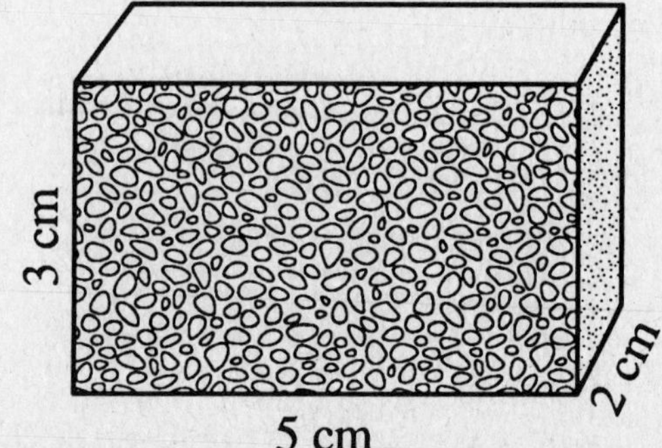

Figure K

6. Centimeter cubes fit perfectly inside the following box. Use the steps below to find the volume of the box.

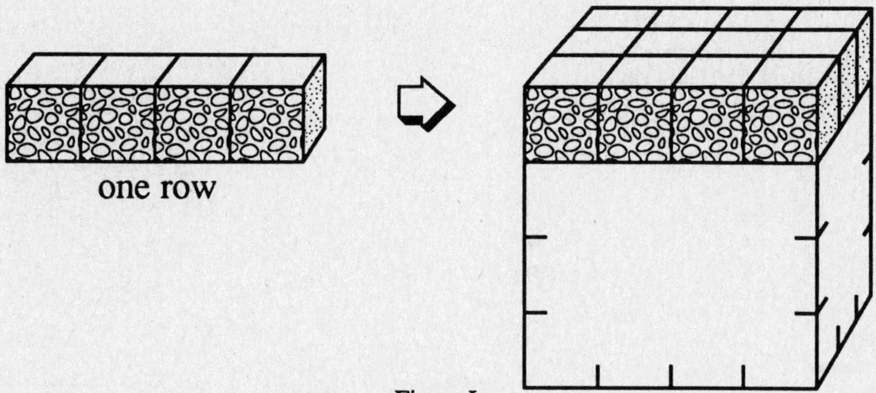

6a. Number of centimeter cubes in one row _______________

6b. Number of rows in one layer _______________

6c. Volume of one layer _______________ cm^3

6d. Number of layers _______________

6e. Volume of box _______________ cm^3

Centimeter cubes are not usually drawn in figures. You can think of the number of centimeter cubes in each row as the **length**, the number of rows in a layer as the **width**, and the number of layers as the **height**.

7. Use the steps below to find the volume of the box at the right. Notice the top layer is shaded.

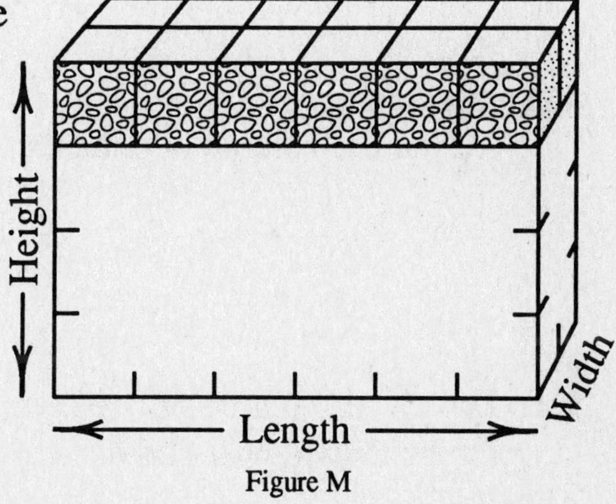

7a. Length _______________ cm

7b. Width _______________ cm

7c. Height _______________ cm

7d. Multiply to find the volume of the box.

Volume _______________ cm^3

8a. How are the boxes in Figures L and M alike? _______________________

8b. How are the boxes different? _______________________________

Sometimes a rectangular box is called a ***rectangular prism*** or a
rectangular parallelepiped.

9. Find the volume of the rectangular parallelepiped
   in the sketch at the right.

   9a. Length _______________ cm

   9b. Width _______________ cm

   9c. Height _______________ cm

   9d. Volume _______________ cm^3

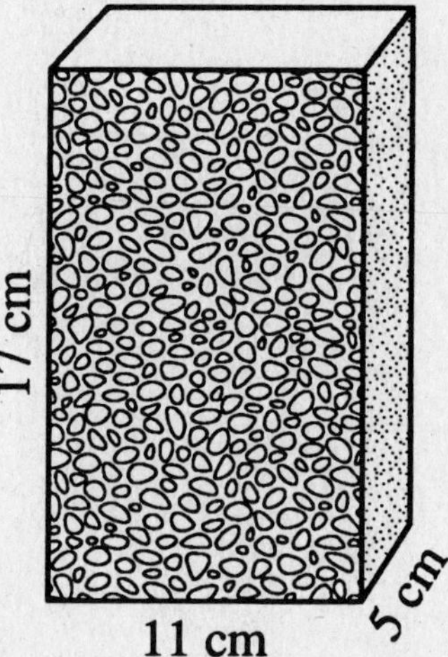

Figure N

If you know the length, width, and height of a box,
you can calculate its volume.

If you know the volume of a box and two of its
dimensions, you can calculate the missing dimension.

---

10. The box at the right is a sketch.
    The total volume of the box is
    48 cm^3. The height of the box
    is 2 cm and the width is 3 cm.
    Find the length using the following
    steps.

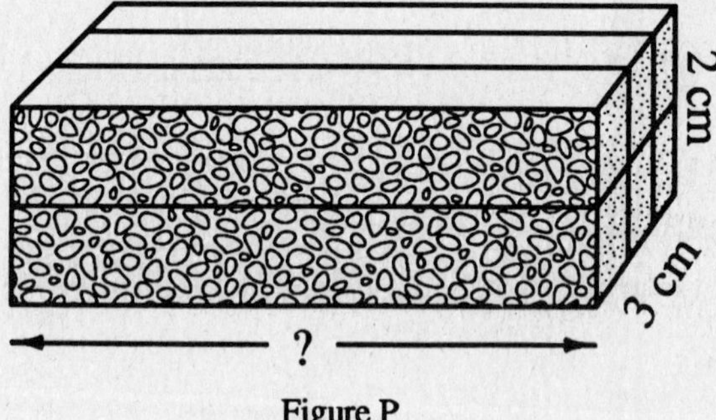

Figure P

10a. Divide the box's volume by its height
     to find the volume of one layer.

     Answer _______________ cm^3

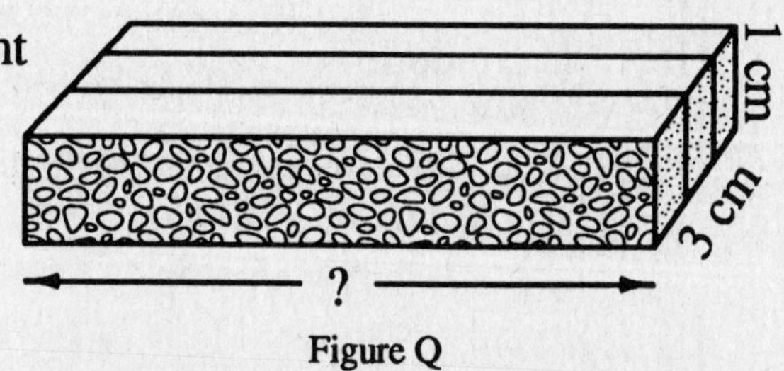

Figure Q

10b. Divide the volume of one layer by
     the box's width to find its length.

     Length _______________ cm

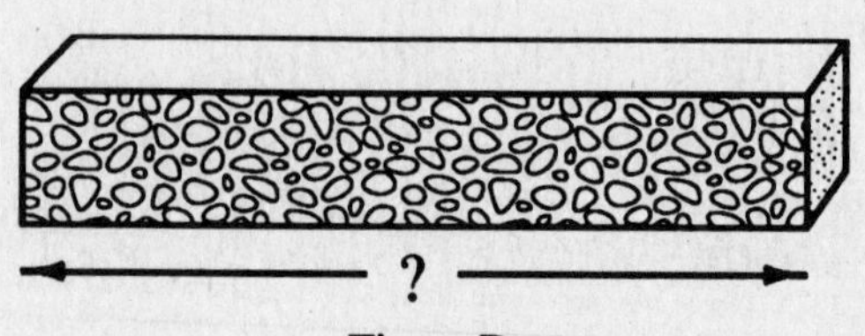

Figure R

11a. The volume of a box is 60 cm^3. If the height is 5 cm, how many centimeter cubes are in each *layer*?

Answer _________________ cubes

11b. There are three rows of cubes in each layer. What is the length of each row?

Length of each row _________________ cm

12. Find the volume of the following boxes.

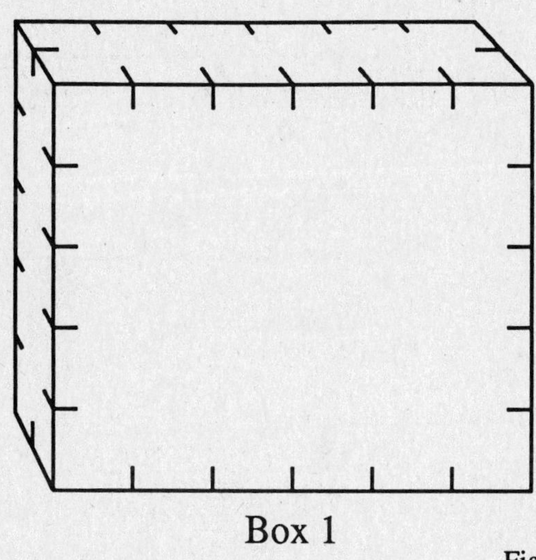
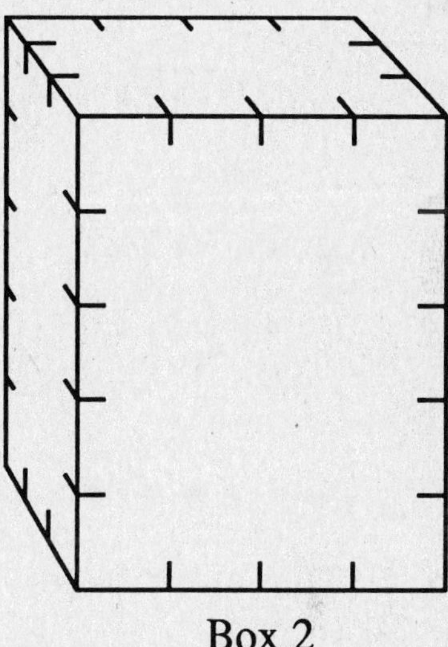

Box 1   Box 2

Figure S

12a. Volume of Box 1 ___________
Put in units.

12b. Volume of Box 2 ___________
Put in units.

12c. Which box, Box 1 or Box 2, is described in Problem 11? ______

★**12d.** Draw a different box with a height of 5 cm and a volume of 60 cm^3. Label the dimensions of your box.

Many times, whole centimeter cubes do not fit exactly in a box.
Each of the following boxes has a volume of 1 cm^3.

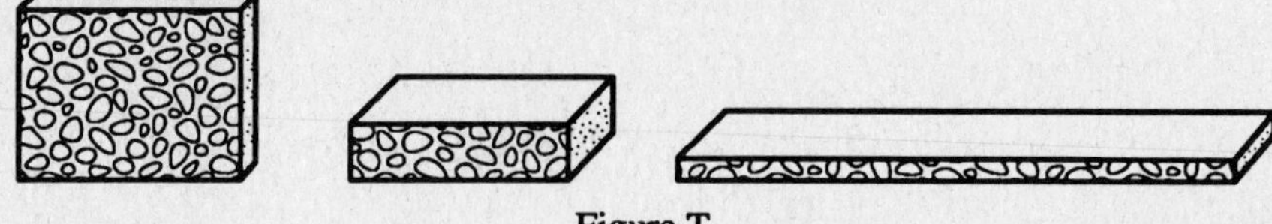

Figure T

These boxes are broken into pieces below. The pieces are put together to form
cubes 1 cm by 1 cm by 1 cm. Even though the boxes have different shapes,
each one has a volume of 1 cm^3.

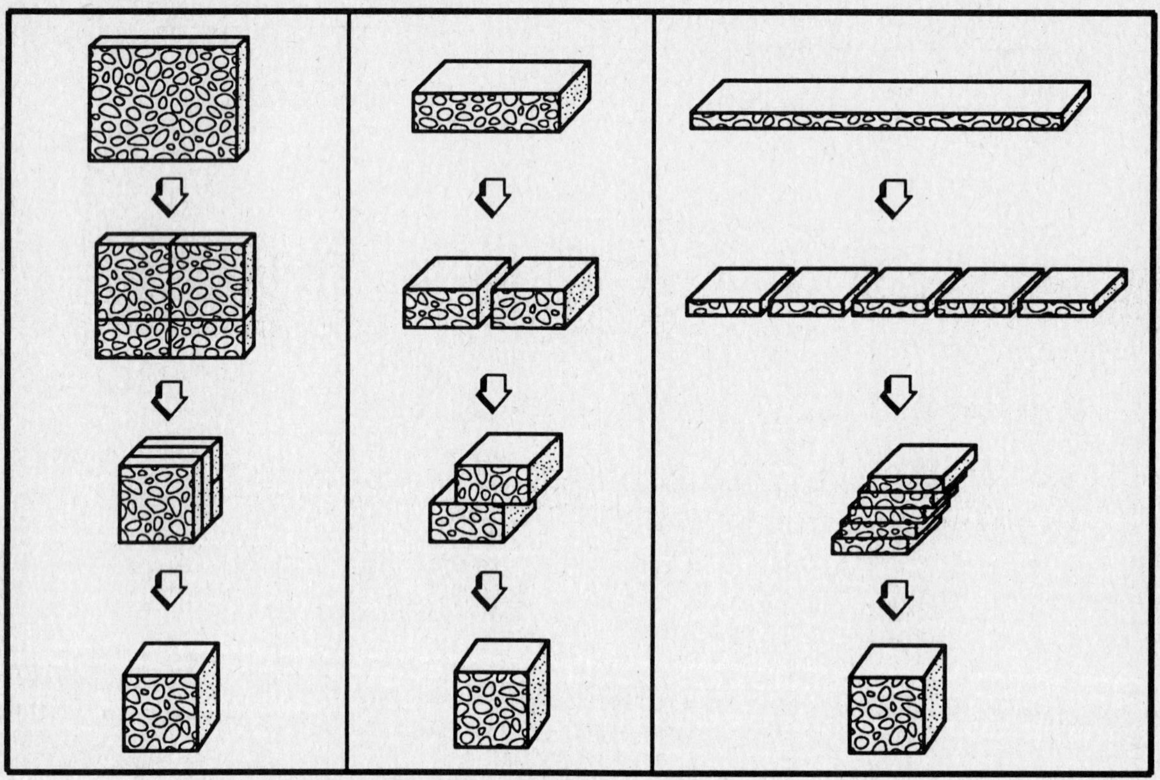

Figure U

Since two pieces like 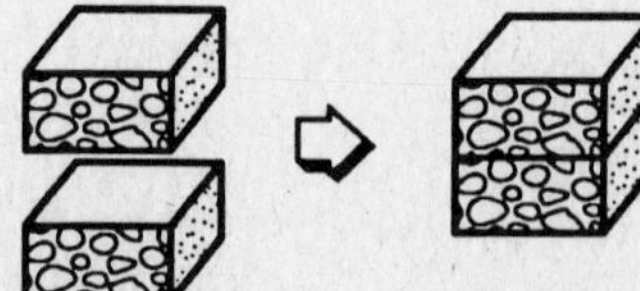 make 1 cm^3, the volume of is $\frac{1}{2}$ cm^3.

Since four pieces like 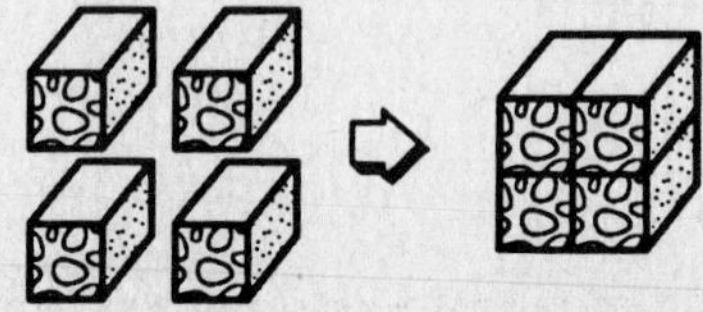 make 1 cm^3, the volume of is $\frac{1}{4}$ cm^3.

13. The box at the right is built from whole and half-centimeter cubes. Find the volume of the box using the steps below.

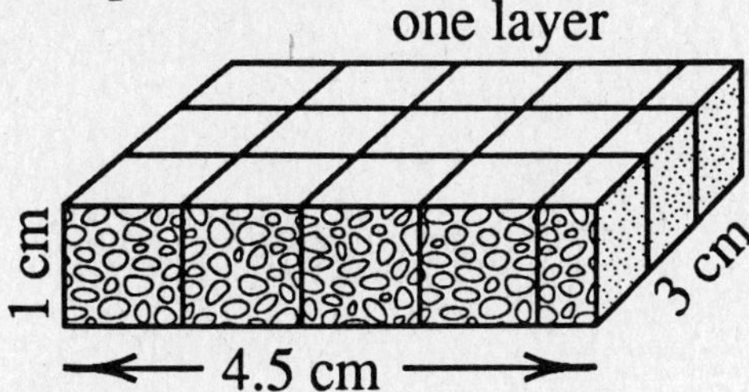

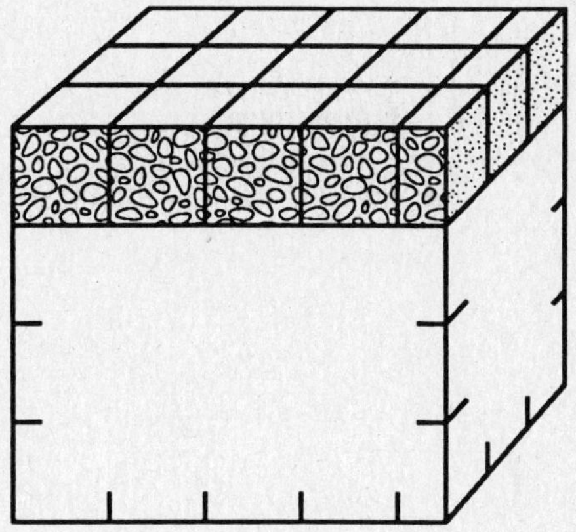

Figure V

13a. Volume of layer ________________
Put in units.

13b. Number of layers ________________

13c. Volume of box ________________
Put in units.

14. Calculate the volume of the following box.

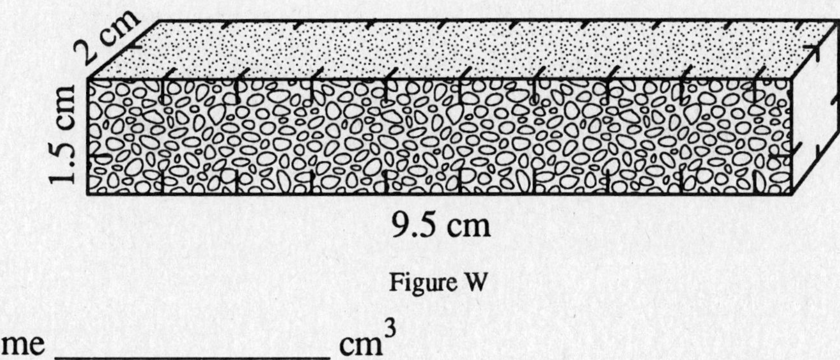

Figure W

Volume ________________ cm^3

15. Calculate the volume of the following box.

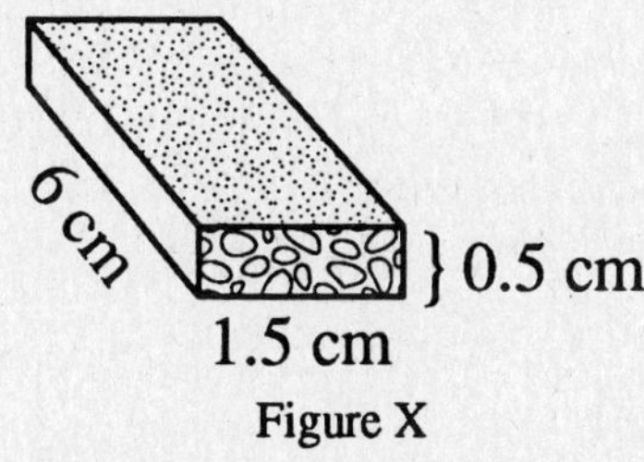

Figure X

Volume ________________
Put in units.

16. Calculate the volume of the boxes in the following sketch.

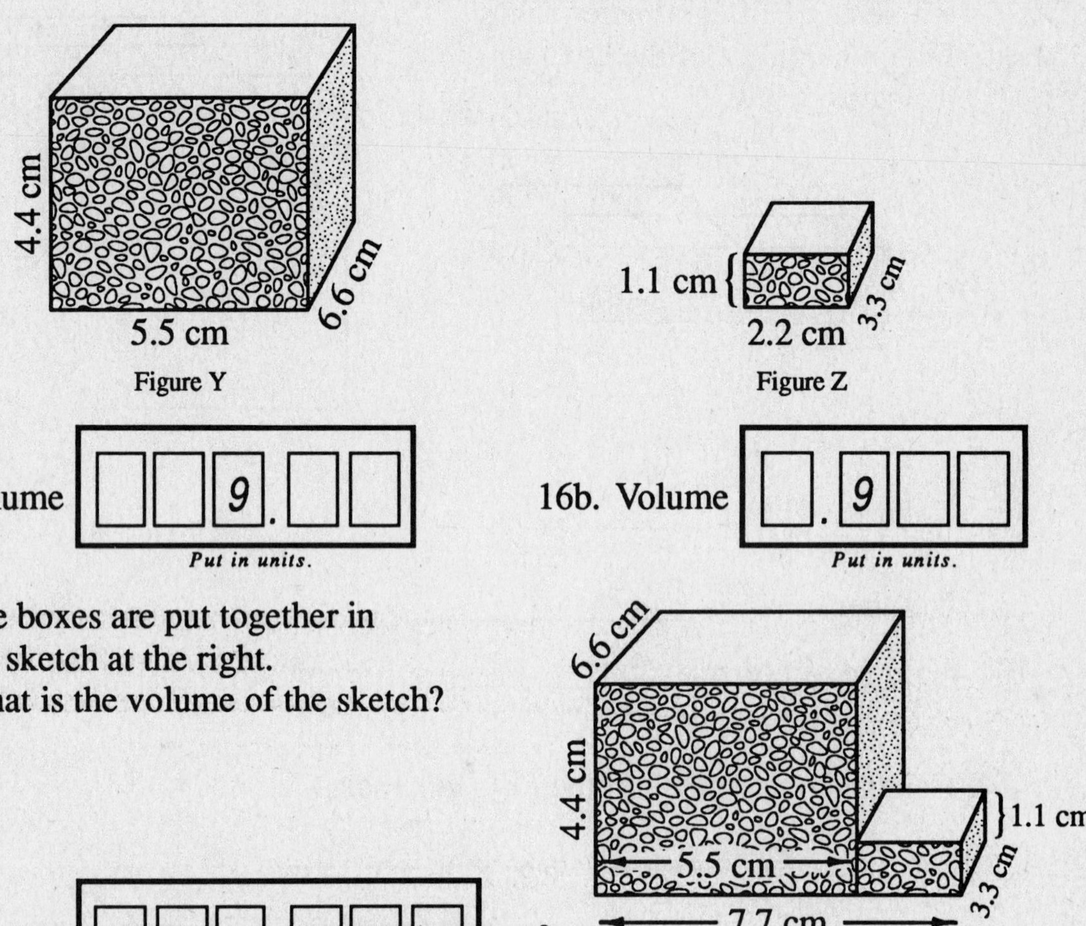

16a. Volume ☐☐9.☐☐
Put in units.

16b. Volume ☐.9☐☐
Put in units.

16c. The boxes are put together in the sketch at the right.
What is the volume of the sketch?

Volume ☐☐7.☐☐☐ cm^3

17a. Two boxes are put together in the following sketch. Write any missing dimensions for each box on the sketch. Calculate the sketch's volume.

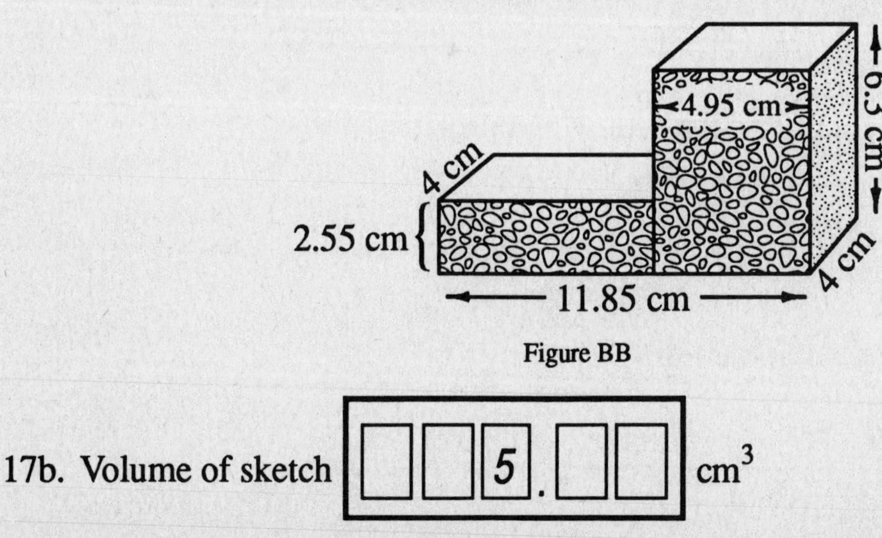

17b. Volume of sketch ☐☐5.☐☐ cm^3

Try It Out!

1. The cube at the right is a sketch.
   Use the following steps to find its volume.

   1a. Length ______________ cm

   1b. Width ______________ cm

   1c. Height ______________
   Put in units.

   1d. Volume ______________
   Put in units.

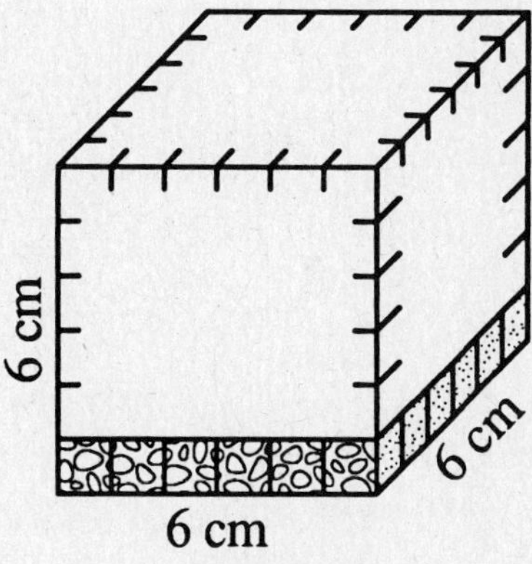

Figure CC

   1e. Complete the following keystrokes that help find the volume of the cube in Figure CC.

6					

In Problem 1e, you multiplied 6 × 6 × 6. When you multiply a number by itself three times, you **cube a number.** Since the three **dimensions** of a cube are the same, there is a quick way to find the volume. To find the volume of a cube, use the $\boxed{y^x}$ (**y to the x**) key.

Be careful! Do **not** use the $\boxed{y^x}$ key to find the volume of a box whose dimensions are different.

---

2. Use the $\boxed{y^x}$ key to find the volume of the cube in Problem 1.

   Press: $\boxed{6}$ $\boxed{y^x}$ $\boxed{3}$ $\boxed{=}$

   Volume ______________ cm^3
   Should agree with Problem 1d.

3a. The cube at the right is a sketch. It has an **edge length** of 23 cm. Use $\boxed{y^x}$ to find its volume.

   Volume ______________ cm^3

3b. List your keystrokes.

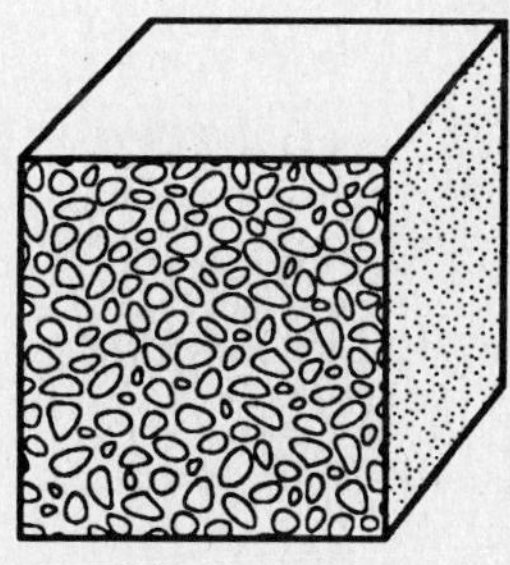

Figure DD

  Maneuvers with Nickels and Numbers

4. What is the volume of a 10 cm cube?

   Volume _________________ cm^3

5. A cube has an edge length of 10.2 cm. Circle your best prediction for the volume of this cube.

   a. The volume of this cube is a little smaller than 1,000 cm^3.

   b. The volume of this cube is much smaller than 1,000 cm^3.

   c. The volume of this cube is 1,000 cm^3.

   d. The volume of this cube is a little larger than 1,000 cm^3.

   e. The volume of this cube is much larger than 1,000 cm^3.

6. Without using your calculator, circle the correct answer for the volume of this cube.

   a. 729 cm^3

   b. 941.192 cm^3

   c. 1,000 cm^3

   d. 1,061.208 cm^3

   e. 1,331 cm^3

7. Now calculate the volume of a 10.2 cm cube.

   Volume _________________ cm^3
   Compare with Problem 6.

8. The edge length of a cube is 4.9731898 cm.
   Complete the following keystrokes to find the volume of this cube.

4.9731898			

   Volume _________________ cm^3
   You'll know.

9. The following figure is built from a white box and a shaded cube.

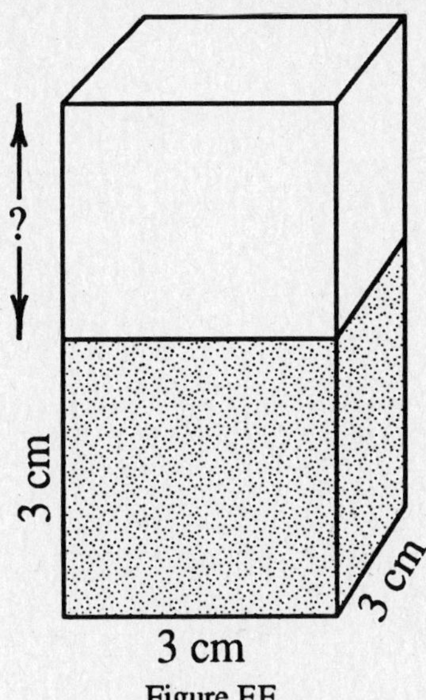

Figure EE

The volume of the figure is 49.5 cm^3. Find the height of the white box using the following steps. Show your work.

9a. Volume of cube _______________ cm^3

9b. Volume of white box _______________ cm^3

9c. Length of white box _______________ cm

9d. Width of white box _______________ cm

9e. Height of white box _______________ cm

10. The sketch at the right is built from two identical cubes and a small white box. The volume of the sketch is 1,985,500 cm^3. Use the following steps to find the height of the white box.

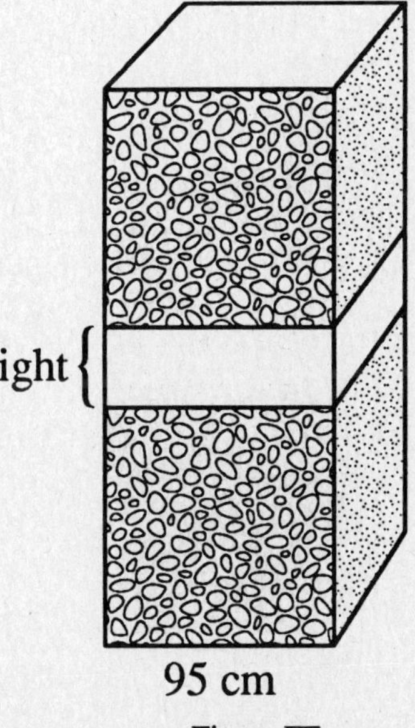

Figure FF

10a. Volume of both cubes _______________ cm^3

10b. Volume of white box _______________ cm^3

10c. Length of white box _______________ cm

10d. Width of white box _______________ cm

10e. Height of white box _______________ cm

                                    Maneuvers with Nickels and Numbers

Homework 4: How Much Room Is in That Box?

1. The following figures are built from centimeter cubes.
   Find the volume of each figure.

1a.

Figure GG

Volume _________________
Put in units.

1b.

Figure HH

Volume _________________
Put in units.

1c.

Figure JJ

Volume _________________
Put in units.

1d.

Figure KK

Volume _________________
Put in units.

1e.

Figure LL

Volume _________________
Put in units.

1f.

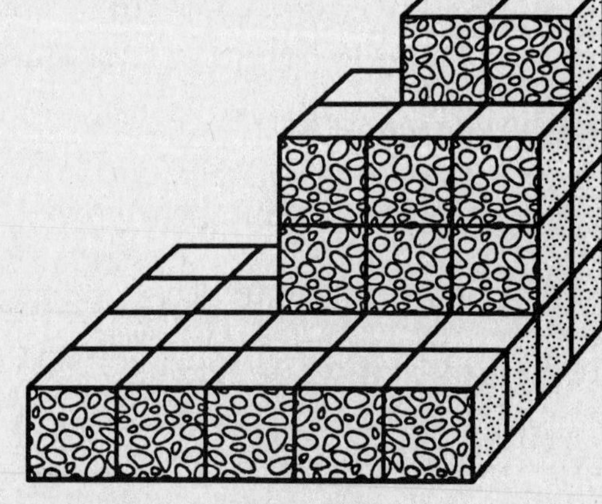

Figure MM

Volume _________________
Put in units.

2. Centimeter cubes fit perfectly in the following box. Find the volume of the box using the steps below.

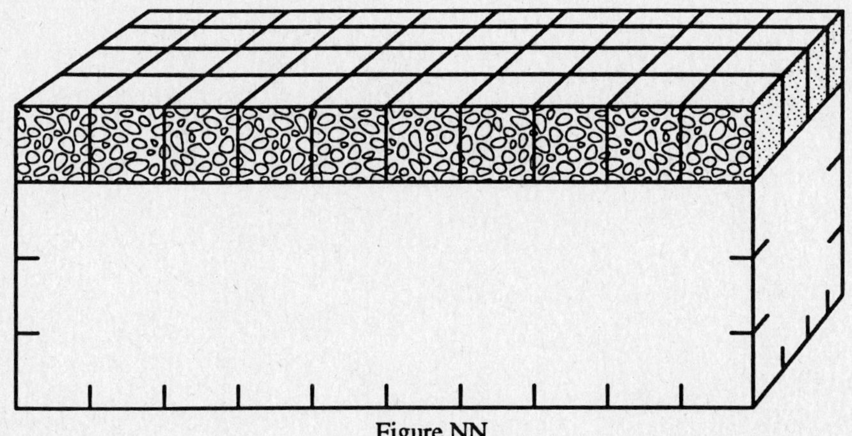

Figure NN

2a. Number of centimeter cubes in one row _________________

2b. Number of rows in a layer _________________

2c. Number of layers _________________

2d. Volume of box _________________ cm^3

3. The volume of the box in the following sketch is 150 cm^3.
   Find the number of centimeter cubes in the shaded layer.
   Then calculate the height of the box.

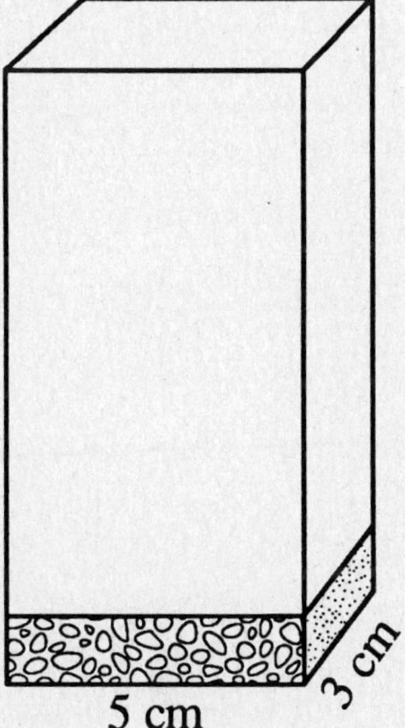

Figure PP

3a. Number of centimeter cubes in each layer _________________

3b. Height _________________ cm

4. Two boxes are put together in the following figure. Calculate the total volume.

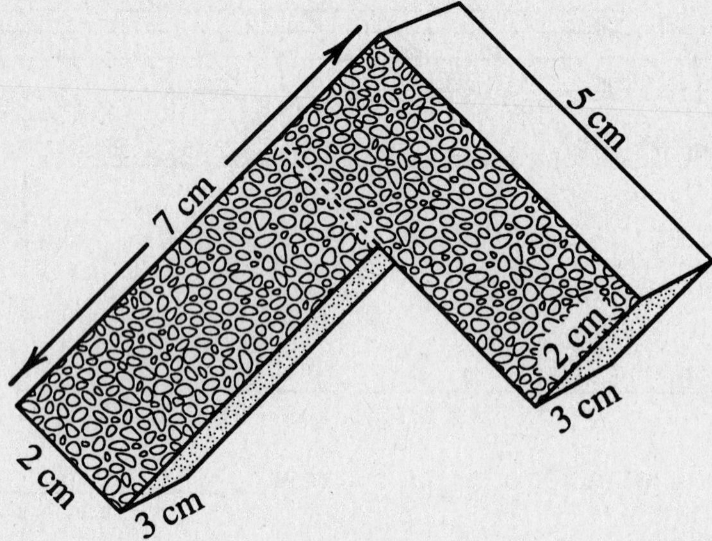

Figure QQ

Total volume _______________
Put in units.

✳ 5. Two boxes are put together in the following figure. The volume of the figure is 36 cm^3. Calculate the width. Show your work.

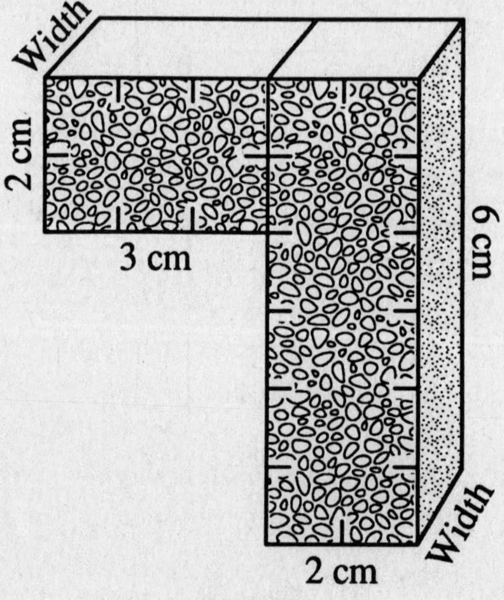

Figure RR

Width _______________
Put in units.

6. Find an object shaped like a box. Make the necessary measurements to calculate the volume of the object.

6a. Object _______________________________________

6b. Dimensions ____________ cm, ____________ cm, ____________ cm
              Length   *Width*   *Height*

6c. Volume ________________
          Put in units.

7. What was the volume of the smallest box measured in your class?

   Answer ________________ cm^3

8. What was the volume of the largest box measured in your class?

   Answer ________________ cm^3

9. The following table shows the volume and two dimensions for six boxes. Calculate the missing dimension. Watch the units.

Box	Length	Width	Height	Volume
A	8 cm	cm	8 cm	448 cm^3
B	25 mm	25 mm	mm	4,375 mm^3
C	0.8 m	m	2 m	1.28 m^3
D	cm	5.5 cm	2.8 cm	200.2 cm^3
E	2 mm	mm	4 mm	24 mm^3
F	5 cm	cm	50 mm *Notice the unit.*	125 cm^3

10. Use the table in Problem 9 to complete Problems 10a through 10e.

10a. Which box is a cube? ____________

10b. Which box can hold *only* one chalkboard eraser? ____________

10c. Which box can hold a refrigerator? ____________

10d. Name the smallest box that can hold three stacked nickels. ____________

10e. What can reasonably fit in Box A? _________________________________

                    Maneuvers with Nickels and Numbers

✱ 11. The following sketch is built from a cube and a white box.
The volume of the figure is 24.276 cm^3.

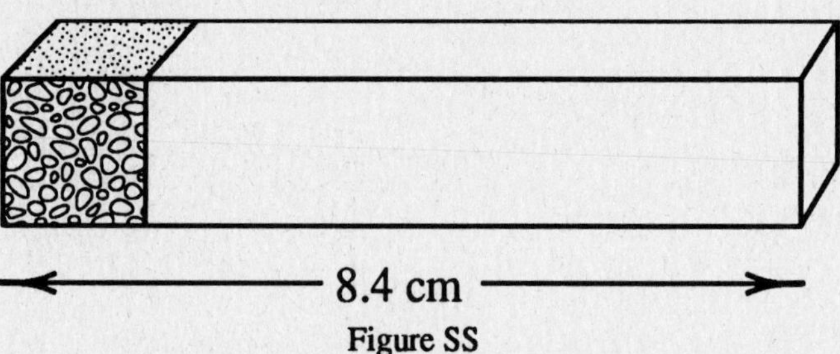

◄———— 8.4 cm ————►

Figure SS

11a. Find the dimensions of the cube. Hint: The width and height of the cube
are the same as the width and height of the figure. Show your work.

Dimensions of cube __________ cm, __________ cm, __________ cm
                     Length   *Width*   *Height*

11b. Volume of cube ☐ . ☐ 1 ☐ cm^3

12. Construction workers built concrete stairs like the following picture.
How many ft.^{3} of concrete did the workers use? Show your work.

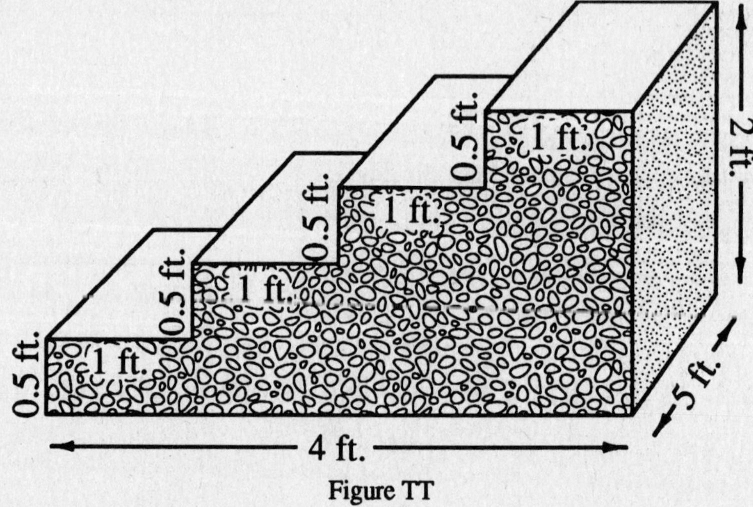

Figure TT

Answer ________________
      Put in units.

5. How Many Nickels Fit in That Box?

In the picture at the right, thousands
of nickels are dropped into a box.
This is called *random packing*.

More nickels may fit in a box if they are neatly stacked. A stack of nickels
forms a cylinder. The following pictures are examples of cylinders.

The following picture shows two ways to arrange stacks of nickels.

Square-cylindrical packing   **Hexagonal-cylindrical packing**

Hexagonal-cylindrical packing allows you to fit a few more nickels in a box;
however, it is easier to calculate volume using square-cylindrical packing.

Use square-cylindrical packing throughout this chapter.

When Pete's Pizzeria delivers a 16-inch pizza, it comes in a box. The bottom of the box is 16 inches by 16 inches. The height of the box is 1.5 inches.

1a. What is the volume of the pizza box?

Volume _________________ in.^{3}

1b. What is the volume of three of these pizza boxes?

Volume _________________ in.^{3}

Since the bottom of the pizza box is a square, we call the box a *Square Packet*.
Imagine a box small enough to hold only one nickel. The bottom of this box is
also a square. The following figure shows the Square Packet for a nickel.

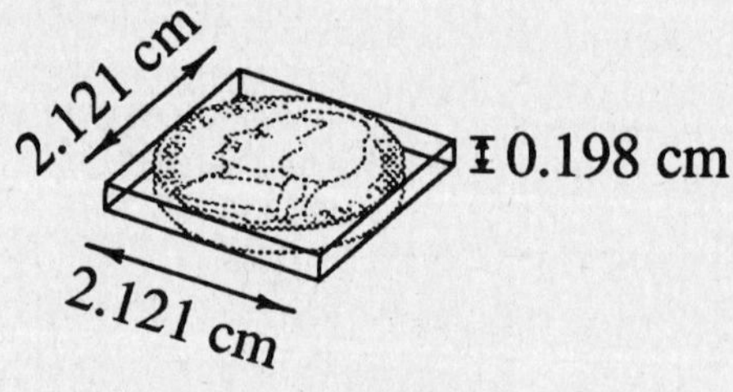

Figure A

2a. List the keystrokes that find the volume of the nickel's Square Packet.

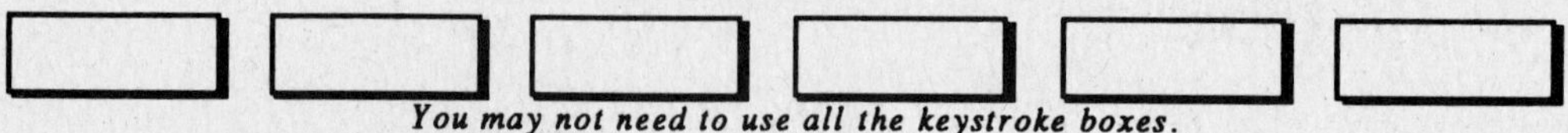

You may not need to use all the keystroke boxes.

2b. Volume ☐ . ☐ 9 cm^3

R to the nearest hundredth.

3. Use the following steps to calculate the volume of four Square Packets of nickels.

3a. Volume of one Square Packet ________________ cm^3

Copy answer from Problem 2b.

3b. Volume of four Square Packets 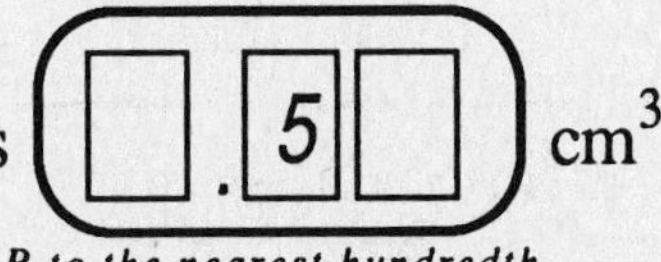 cm^3

R to the nearest hundredth.

4. Find the volume of four Square Packets of nickels another way. The diameter of a nickel is 2.121 cm and its height is 0.198 cm. Use the following steps to calculate the volume of the box at the right.

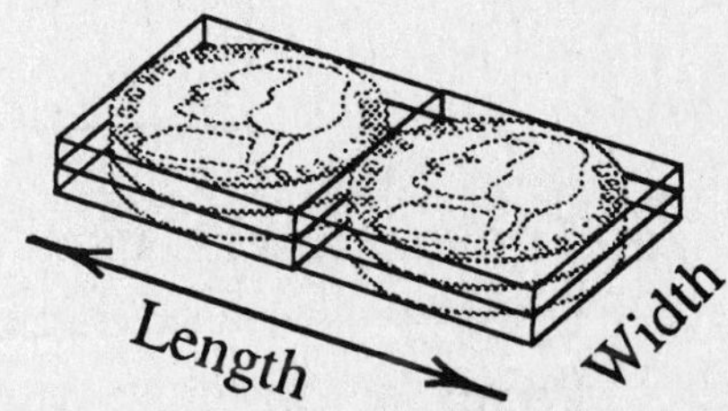

Figure B

4a. Length ________________ cm

4b. Width ________________

Put in units.

4c. Height ________________

Put in units.

4d. Volume  cm^3

R to the nearest hundredth.

4e. If Problem 4d does not agree with Problem 3b, go back and check your work.

5a. Eight Square Packets of nickels fit in the box at the right. Use any method to calculate the volume of the box.

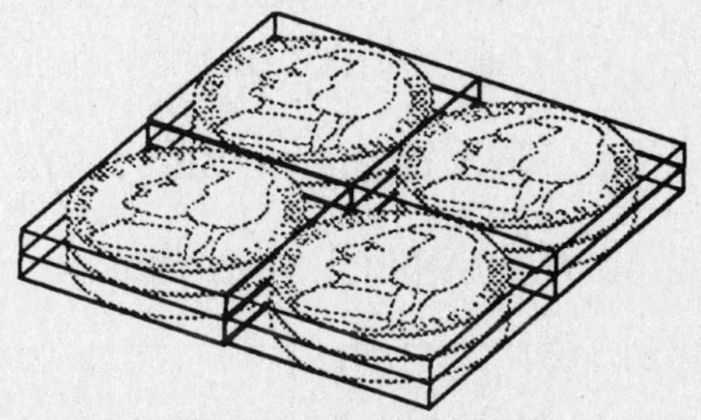

Figure C

Volume 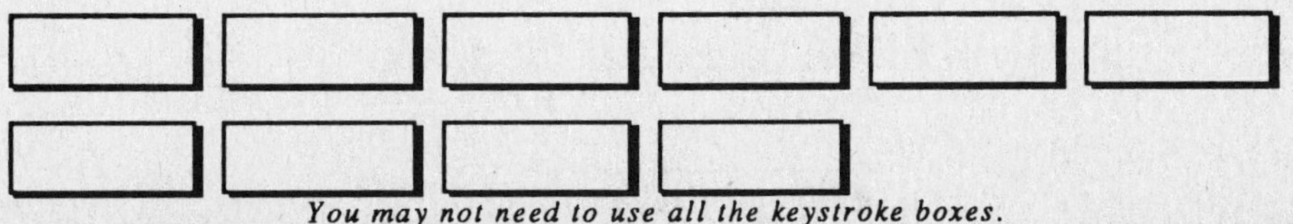 cm^3

R to the nearest tenth.

5b. List the keystrokes you used to solve Problem 5a.

You may not need to use all the keystroke boxes.

6. Complete the following table. Remember, the volume of a nickel's
   Square Packet is 0.89 cm^3.

Number of Nickel Square Packets	Volume
1	0.89 cm^3
10	cm^3
50	cm^3
100	cm^3

7a. Twelve nickel packets fit in a box.
    Draw a sketch of this box at the right.
    Label the dimensions of the box.

7b. Calculate the volume of this box.

   Volume _________________ cm^3

7c. Many different boxes can be drawn for
    Problem 7a. How many can you draw?

   Answer _______________ boxes

7d. Is the volume the same for these different boxes? ________________
   Yes or No

   Why or why not? ____

8. Nickel packets form the stack at the right.
   The volume of this stack is 14.24 cm^3.

8a. How many nickels form the stack? ________________

8b. List your keystrokes for Problem 8a.

   [] [] [] []

Figure D

9. Nickel packets form a stack.
   The stack's volume is 109.47 cm^3.
   Calculate the number of nickel packets in the stack.

   Number of nickel packets _______________
   You'll know.

10. Monique has a 12 cm cube like the sketch at the right.

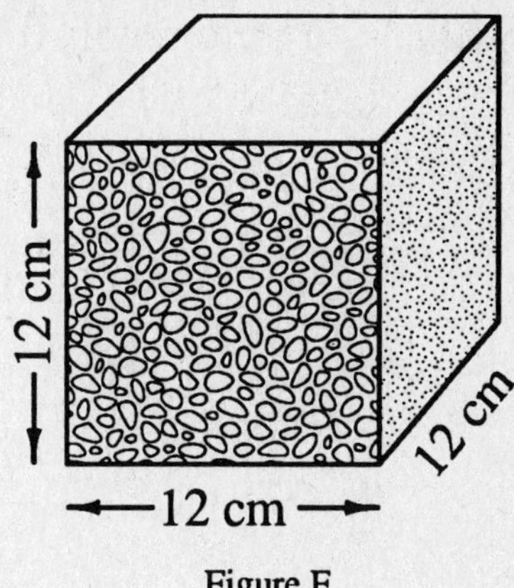

10a. What is the volume of this cube?

Volume ________________
Put in units.

10b. How many nickel packet volumes does it take to equal the volume of the cube?

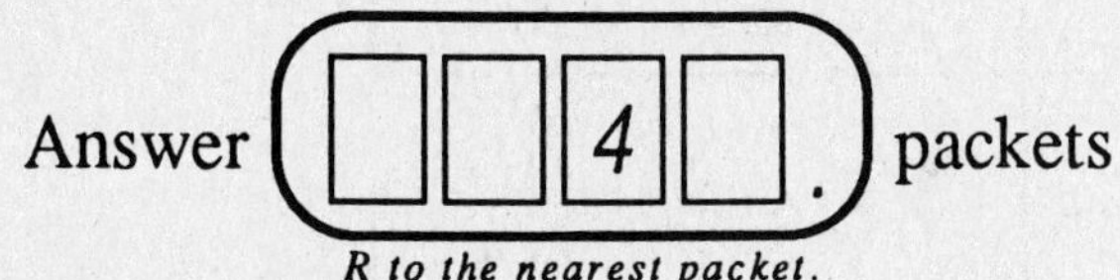

Answer (□ □ 4 □ .) packets
R to the nearest packet.

This is a good estimate of the number of square-packed nickels that will fit in the cube.

11a. Tyrone has a cube with a volume of 2,744 cm^3. Find the edge length of Tyrone's cube by trial and error using $\boxed{y^x}$. Fill in the missing units in the table.

Edge Length	Volume *You want 2,744 cm³.*
13 cm	2,197 cm^3 *Too small.*
20 cm	8,000 cm^3 *Too big.*
What is your next try?	*Too big or too small?*
What is your next try?	*Too big or too small?*
What is your next try?	*Too big or too small?*
What is your next try?	*Too big or too small?*

11b. Use the volume of a nickel packet to estimate the number of nickels that will fit in Tyrone's cube.

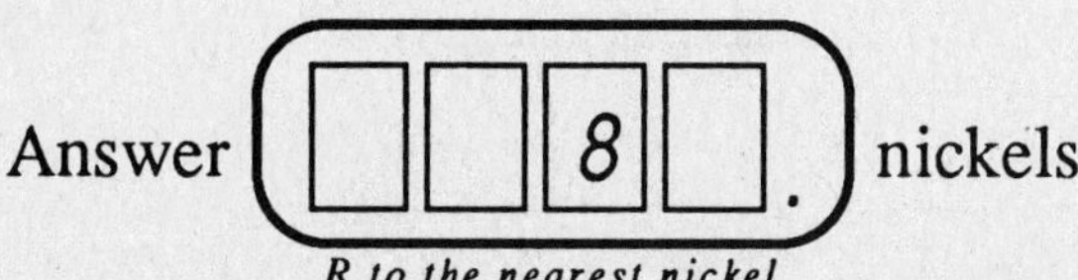

Answer (□ □ 8 □ .) nickels
R to the nearest nickel.

12a. The volume of Anthony's cube is 3,048.625 cm^3. Use trial and error and $\boxed{y^x}$ to find the edge length of the cube. Fill in the missing units.

Edge Length	Volume *You want 3,048.625 cm^3.*
10 cm	1,000 cm^3 *Too small.*
What is your next try?	*Too big or too small?*
What is your next try?	*Too big or too small?*
What is your next try?	*Too big or too small?*
What is your next try?	*Too big or too small?*
What is your next try?	*Too big or too small?*

Edge length of cube _________________ cm

12b. Use the volume of a nickel packet to estimate the number of nickels that will fit in Anthony's cube.

Answer _________________ nickels
R to the nearest nickel.

13. The volume of a cube is 18,609.625 cm^3. Find the edge length of the cube by trial and error. Fill in the missing units.

Edge Length	Volume *You want 18,609.625 cm^3.*
40 cm	*Too big or too small?*

Edge length of cube _________________ cm

> There is a faster way to find the edge length of a cube when you know its volume.
>
> Look at $\sqrt[x]{y}$ directly above the $\boxed{y^x}$ key on your calculator. This is called the **xth root**. Use $\sqrt[x]{y}$ to find the cube root. If you know the volume of a cube, the cube root is the edge length of the cube.
>
> Press $\boxed{\text{INV}}$ to change $\boxed{y^x}$ into $\sqrt[x]{y}$.
> For example, the volume of a cube is 18,609.625 cm^3.
> To find the edge length, press: $\boxed{18609.625}$ $\boxed{\text{INV}}$ $\boxed{y^x}$ $\boxed{3}$ $\boxed{=}$.
>
> Answer ________________ cm
> *Should agree with*
> *Problem 13.*
>
> This 3 gives you the cube root.
>
> $\sqrt[3]{18,609.625} = 26.5$, since $26.5 \times 26.5 \times 26.5 = 18,609.625$.

14a. Find the cube root of 1,331. ________________

14b. Complete the following keystrokes.

$\boxed{1331}$ $\boxed{}$ $\boxed{y^x}$ $\boxed{}$ $\boxed{=}$

15. Find the cube root of 704,969. ________________

16. A cube has a volume of 700 cm^3.

16a. List your keystrokes to find its edge length.

$\boxed{}$ $\boxed{}$ $\boxed{}$ $\boxed{}$ $\boxed{}$

16b. Edge length $\boxed{} . \boxed{8} \boxed{} \boxed{9} \boxed{} \boxed{}$ cm

16c. How can you check this to be sure? ________________________________

17a. The volume of a cube is 729 cm^3. Is the edge length of the cube more or less than Problem 16b?

Answer ________________
More or Less

17b. Calculate the edge length of the cube. ________________ cm

                              Maneuvers with Nickels and Numbers

Try It Out!

1. Use the following steps to estimate the edge length of a cube needed to hold $1,000 worth of square-packed nickels.

1a. How many nickels are in $1,000?

Answer _________________ nickels

1b. Calculate the volume of $1,000 worth of nickel packets. The volume of one nickel's Square Packet is 0.89 cm^3.

Volume of $1,000 _________________ cm^3

1c. Imagine a cube that has the same volume as $1,000 of nickel packets. Calculate the edge length of this cube.

Edge length _________________ cm
R to the nearest cm.

2. Which is the smallest "box" that you think could hold $1,000 worth of nickels? Check your best guess below.

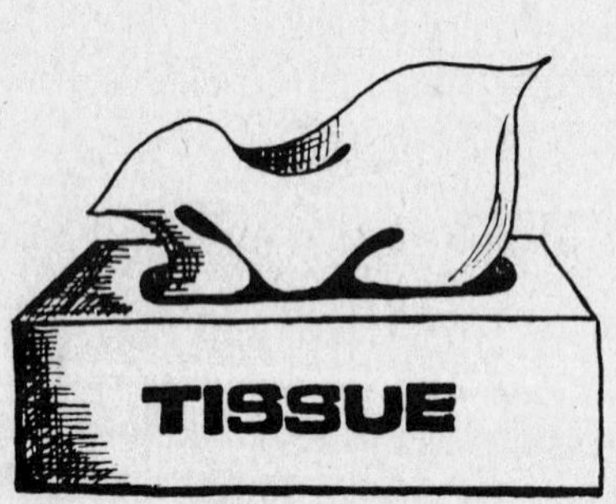

______ Tissue box   ______ Cereal box

______ School desk   ______ Closet

3. Measure the following objects. Then find the volume of each object.

Object	Length	Width	Height	Volume
Tissue box	cm	cm	cm	cm^3
Cereal box	cm	cm	cm	cm^3
School desk	cm	cm	cm	cm^3
Closet	cm	cm	cm	cm^3

4. Circle the smallest "box" in Problem 3 that can hold $1,000.

5. The base of a tissue box is 24 cm by 12 cm. The height of the box is 4.5 cm. Find an estimated value for the number of square-packed nickels that fit in this tissue box using the following steps.

5a. What is the volume of the tissue box?

Volume [ ] [ ] [9] [ ] . cm^3

5b. How many nickel packet volumes are in the tissue box? Remember, the volume of a nickel packet is 0.89 cm^3.

Answer ([ ] [4] [5] [ ] .) packet volumes

R to the nearest packet.

5c. What is the dollar value? $_______________

6. In Problem 5, you found an estimated value for the number of nickels in the tissue box. Find the exact number using the following steps.

6a. On a sheet of paper, draw the bottom of the tissue box (24 cm by 12 cm). Square pack one layer of nickels in the rectangle.

6b. How many whole nickels fit along the length? _______________

6c. How many whole nickels fit along the width? _______________

6d. How many whole nickels fit in one layer? _______________

6e. The height of the tissue box is 4.5 cm. The official height of one nickel is
0.198 cm. How many whole nickels will be in each stack?
Show your work.

Answer ________________ nickels

6f. How many whole nickels fit in this tissue box?

Answer | | 2 | 1 | |. nickels

6g. What is the dollar value? $________________

7. Compare Problem 5b with Problem 6f. Is the exact number of nickels
more or less than the estimate?

Answer ________________
More or Less

Why? ____

8. Find an estimated number of nickel packets that fit in the tissue box you
measured in the table on page 67. Show your work.

Answer ________________ packets
R to the nearest packet.

9. Find the exact number of square-packed nickels that fit in your tissue box.
Show your work.

Answer ________________ nickels

Homework 5: How Many Nickels Fit in That Box?

1. Complete the following table. Use $\boxed{y^x}$ and $\boxed{\text{INV}}\,\boxed{y^x}$.

	Edge Length of Cube	Volume
1a.	3.6840315 cm	cm³ *You'll know.*
1b.	cm *R to the nearest hundredth.*	1,001 cm³
1c.	21 cm	cm³
1d.	cm	27,000 cm³

2a. The box at the right is a sketch. What is the volume of this box?

Volume _____________ cm³
Copy window.

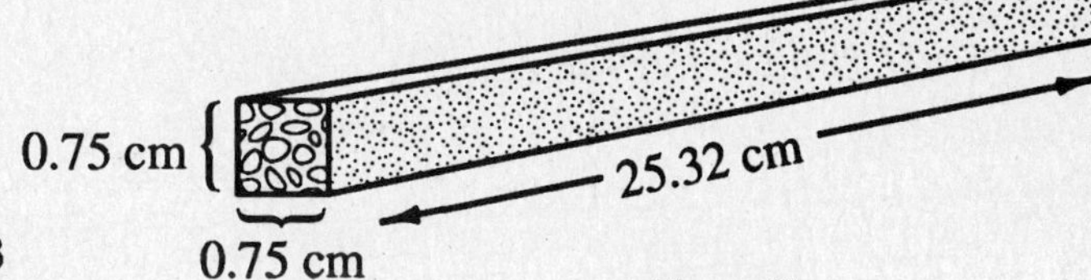

2b. Does this box have a large enough volume for 16 nickel packets? _________
Yes or No

2c. If you said "yes," you are right, but look at Figure F again.
How many nickel packets would *really fit* in this box? _____________

Why? ____

3. Calculate the volume of a Square Packet for each coin in the following table.

	Coin	Diameter	Thickness *Notice the unit.*	Volume of Packet *R to the nearest hundredth.*
3a.	Quarter	2.426 cm	1.75 mm	cm³
3b.	Dime	1.791 cm	1.35 mm	cm³
3c.	Nickel	2.121 cm	1.98 mm	0.89 cm³
3d.	Penny	1.905 cm	1.57 mm	cm³

4. Imagine cubes that have the same volume as $1,000 worth of each coin. Predict the size of these "$1,000 cubes" by answering the following questions. Circle the cube that you predict has a larger volume.

4a. $1,000 worth of pennies   or $1,000 worth of dimes

Explain. ____

4b. $1,000 worth of dimes   or $1,000 worth of nickels

Explain. ____

4c. $1,000 worth of quarters   or $1,000 worth of dimes

Explain. ____

4d. Use your predictions to rank the cubes from largest to smallest.

_______________ _______________ _______________ _______________
   Largest Cube   *Smallest Cube*

5. Calculate the edge length of the "$1,000 cubes" in the following table.

Coin	Volume of Square Packet	Number of Packets in $1,000	Volume of $1,000 *R to the nearest tenth.*	Edge Length of Cube *R to the nearest tenth.*
Quarter	cm³		cm³	cm
Dime	cm³		cm³	cm
Nickel	cm³		cm³	cm
Penny	cm³		cm³	cm

6. Use your calculations in Problem 5 to rank the "$1,000 cubes" from largest to smallest. Compare your calculations with your predictions in Problem 4d.

_______________ _______________ _______________ _______________
   Largest Cube   *Smallest Cube*

7a. The base of a box is 8 cm by 8 cm. Its height is 18 cm.
Estimate the number of quarter packets that fit in this box. ___________

7b. How many quarter packets will actually fit in this box? ______________

6. How Much Wrapping Paper Do I Need?

1. Follow Steps **a** through **c** to build a cube using the pattern at the bottom of the page.

   a. Cut along the dark solid lines.

   b. Fold the paper along the dashed lines.

   c. Tape the sides together.

   When you are finished, your cube will look like the one at the right.

Figure A

2. What are the dimensions of the cube you built?

2a. Length _______________ cm

2b. Width _______________ cm

2c. Height _______________ cm

- Cut below this line. -

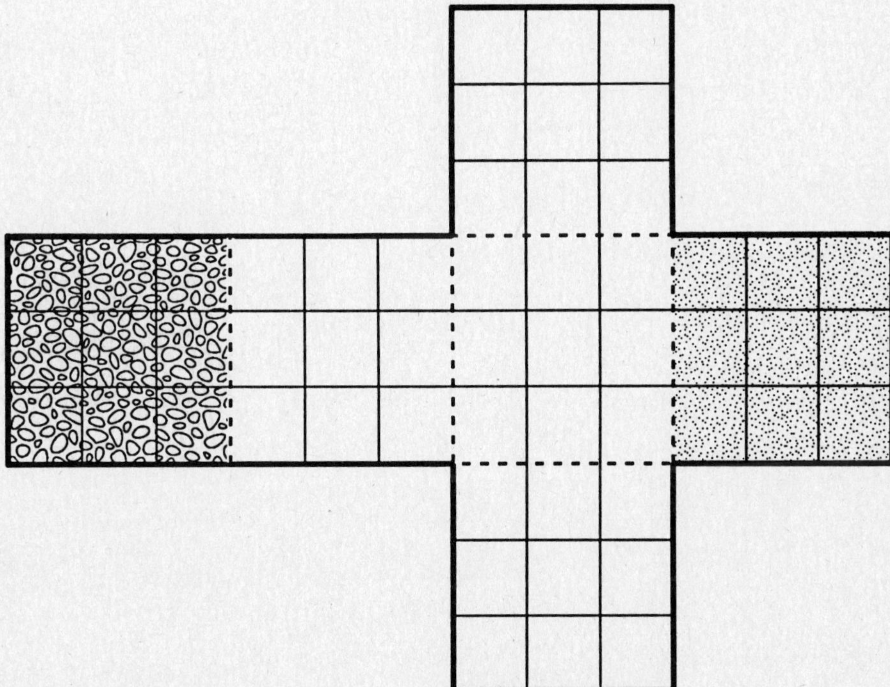

Figure B

     Maneuvers with Nickels and Numbers

All the dimensions or *edge lengths* of any cube are the same. The edge of the cube you built is 3 cm.

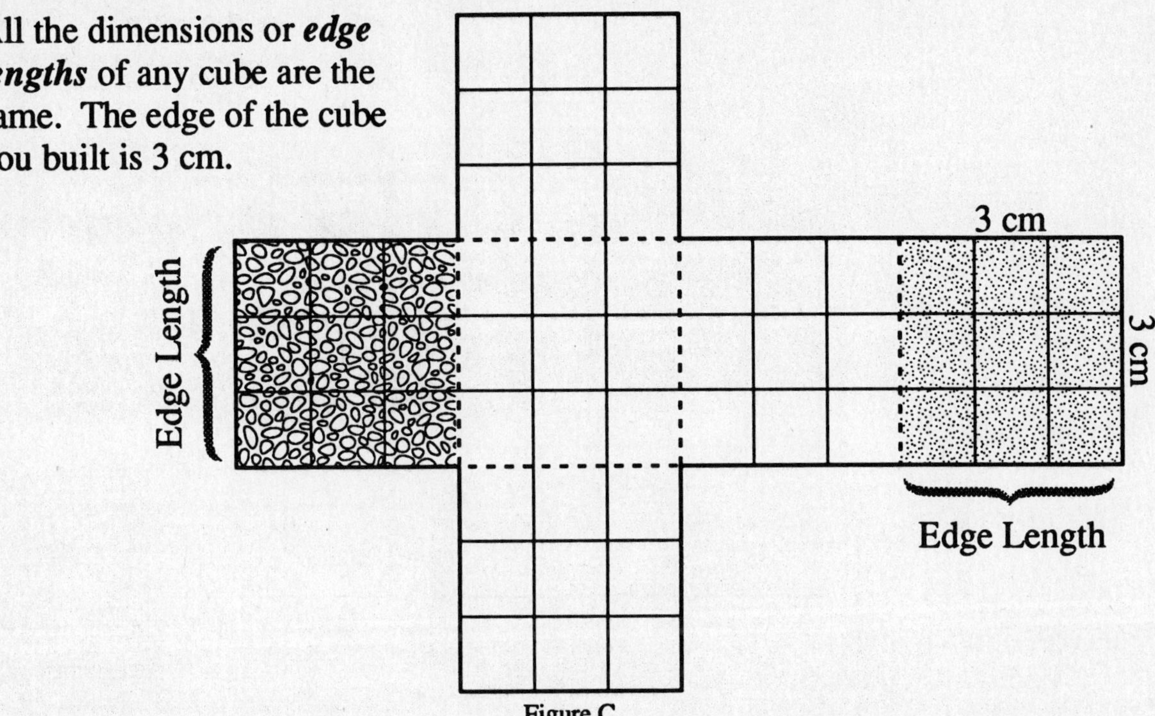

3. Each side of a cube is called a *face*. How many faces does a cube have?

   Answer ________________ faces

4. Each face on a cube is a square. What is the area of one of the squares?

   Area ________________ cm^2

The total area of all six faces is called the *surface area* of the cube. Imagine perfectly covering a cube with six pieces of wrapping paper. The total area of the wrapping paper would equal the surface area of the cube.

To find the surface area of the cube, add up the area of all the faces.

5. What is the surface area of the cube you built? ________________ cm^2

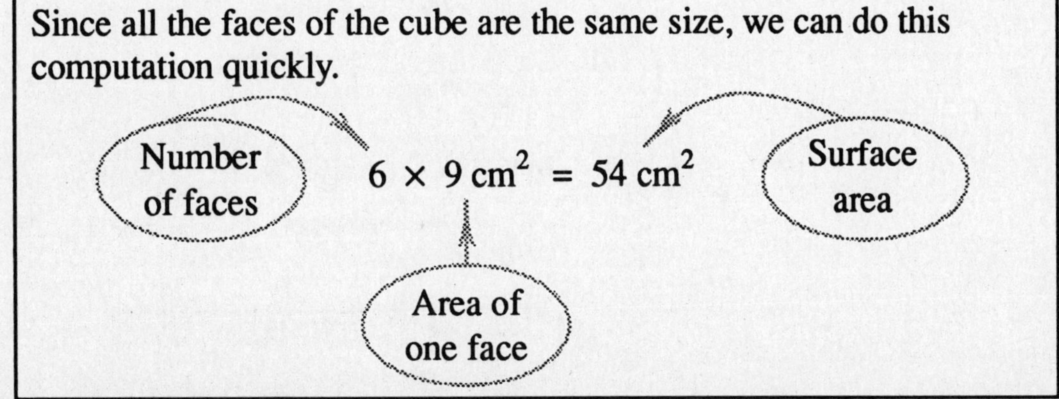

Since all the faces of the cube are the same size, we can do this computation quickly.

                                        Maneuvers with Nickels and Numbers

6. Look at the following 5 cm cube.

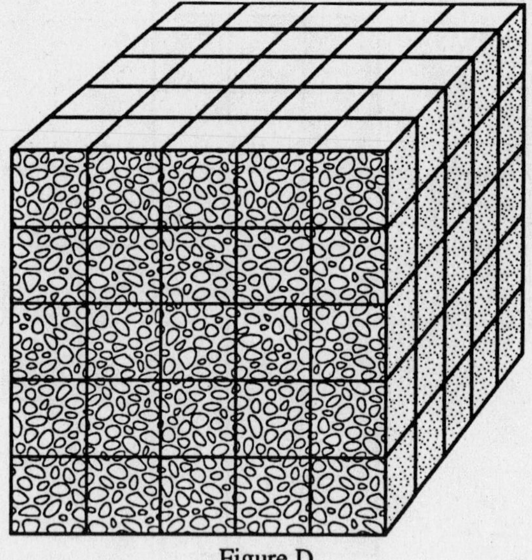

Figure D

6a. What is the area of one face? _________________ cm^2

6b. What number do you multiply by to find the surface area of a cube? _____

6c. What is the surface area? _________________ cm^2

6d. Alice's answer for Problem 6c is 125 cm^2. What did Alice actually find?

____

The *edge length* of the cube above is measured in *cm*.
Square centimeters (cm^2) are used to measure its *surface area*.
Cubic centimeters (cm^3) are used to measure its *volume*.

7. Explain the difference between the surface area and the volume of a cube.

____

____

8a. Find the surface area of the 2 cm cube
at the right.

Surface area _________________ cm^2

8b. List the keystrokes you used for Problem 8a.

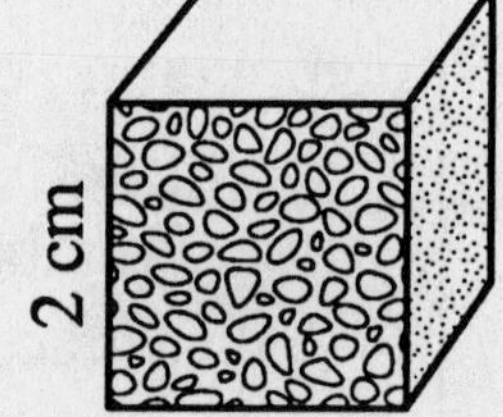

Figure E

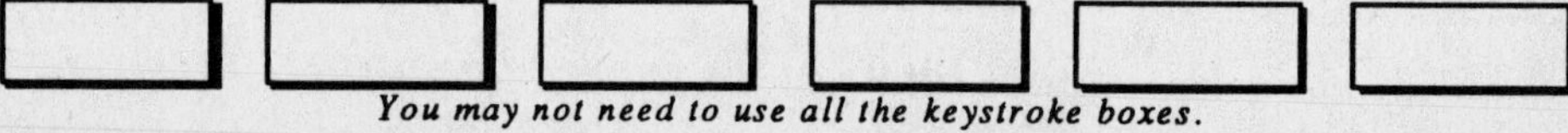

You may not need to use all the keystroke boxes.

9. Complete the following table. Fill in the missing units.

	Edge Length of Cube	Area of One Face	Surface Area
9a.	10 cm		cm^2
9b.	12 cm		
9c.	14.341083 cm	cm^2 *Copy window.*	*You'll know.*
9d.	15 cm		

10. The *surface area* of the cube in the sketch at the right is 600 cm^2.

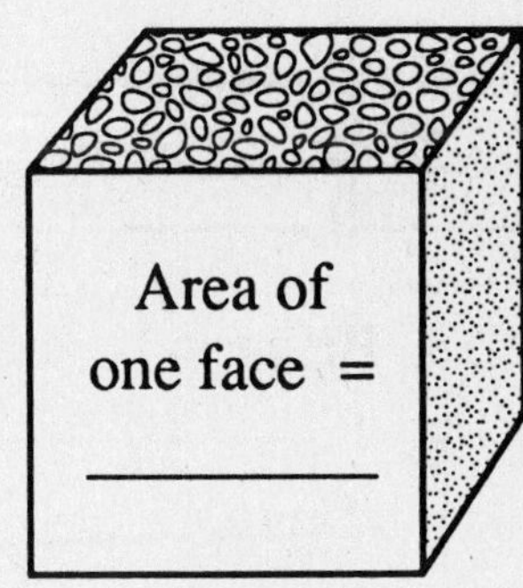

Figure F

10a. Find the area of one face.

Area of one face __________________
Put in units.

When you know the area of a square,
use INV $\sqrt{x}$ to find the edge length of that square.

10b. Press: 100 INV $\sqrt{x}$

10c. Window: ☐☐.
Edge length

10d. Starting with the surface area of the cube, list the keystrokes needed to find the edge length in one run.

11. The surface area of a cube is 2,400 cm^2. Find the edge length using the following steps.

11a. Area of one face __________________ cm^2

11b. Edge length __________________ cm

11c. List your keystrokes.

 12. Complete the following table. Fill in the missing units.

	Edge Length of Cube	Area of One Face	Surface Area
12a.	3.5355339 cm		*You'll know.*
12b.	☐.☐☐☐☐4 5☐ cm		96.3 cm^2
12c.			486 cm^2
12d.		625 cm^2	
12e.			15,000 cm^2

13. Bring in boxes from home. Complete the following table.

Type of Box	Dimensions (in cm)	Surface Area	Volume
		cm^2	cm^3
		cm^2	cm^3
		cm^2	cm^3
		cm^2	cm^3
		cm^2	cm^3
		cm^2	cm^3

13a. Do any of the boxes have approximately the same surface area? __________

Yes or No

Which boxes? ____

13b. Do any of the boxes have approximately the same volume? __________

Yes or No

Which boxes? ____

14. The surface area of the cube you built on page 71 is 54 cm^2. Find its volume using the following steps.

14a. Area of one face _______________ cm^2

14b. Edge length _______________
     Put in units.

14c. Volume _______________ cm^3

14d. List the keystrokes for Problem 14.

54								

Figure G

15. The surface area of a cube is 1,014 cm^2. Draw a sketch of this cube. Calculate its edge length and volume.

15a. Edge length _______________
     Put in units.

15b. Volume _______________
     Put in units.

16. The surface area of a cube is 950.85257 cm^2. Calculate its volume. List your keystrokes.

Volume _______________ cm^3
        You'll know.

17. The volume of the cube you built on page 71 is 27 cm^3. Find the surface area using the following steps.

17a. Edge length _______________
     Put in units.

17b. Area of one face _______________ cm^2

17c. Surface area _______________ cm^2
     Should agree with Problem 5.

17d. List the keystrokes you used for Problem 17.

27	INV							

If you know any fact about the size of a cube, you can calculate anything else about that cube.

18. Complete the following table. Fill in the missing units.

	Edge Length of Cube	Volume	Surface Area
18a.	21 cm	cm^3	cm^2
18b.		10,648 cm^3	
18c.	*Michael Jordan's number*		3,174 cm^2
18d.		13,824 cm^3	

19. The volume of a cube is 343 cm^3. Calculate the surface area. Show your work.

Surface area ________________
  Put in units.

20a. The volume of a cube is 340 cm^3. Circle your best prediction for the surface area of the cube. Hint: Look at Problem 19.

  a. The surface area is a little smaller than 294 cm^2.
  b. The surface area is much smaller than 294 cm^2.
  c. The surface area is 294 cm^2.
  d. The surface area is a little larger than 294 cm^2.
  e. The surface area is much larger than 294 cm^2.

20b. Without using your calculator, circle the correct surface area of the cube.

  a. 487.28321 cm^2
  b. 295.63428 cm^2
  c. 294 cm^2
  d. 292.28321 cm^2
  e. 157.25832 cm^2

21. Now calculate the surface area to check your answer.

Surface area ________________ cm^2
  Copy window.

Try It Out!

1. Predict which patterns below will fold to make a cube. Try to "fold them" in your head.

   Answers ________________

2. Cut out the patterns and build the cubes to check your predictions. Which patterns will fold to make a cube?

   Answers ________________

3. Pattern E doesn't build a cube. Why not? ______________________________

- Cut below this line. -

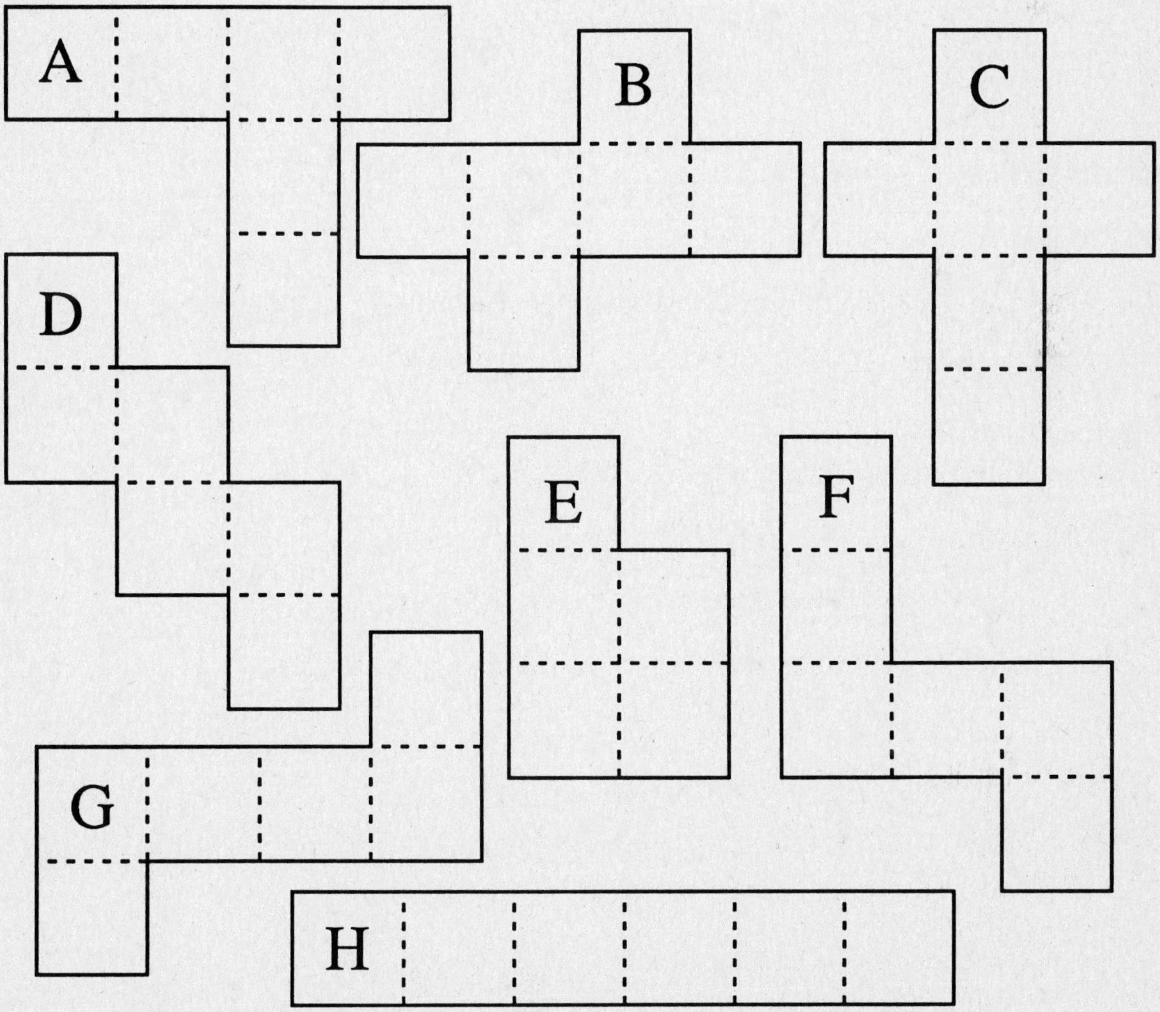

Figure H

4. The cube in Figure J is a sketch. Calculate the surface area and volume of the cube.

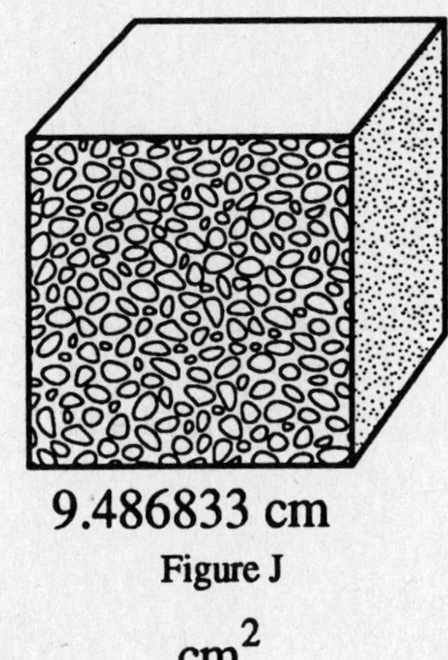

9.486833 cm

Figure J

4a. Surface area ________________ cm^2

You'll know.

4b. Volume [ ][ ][ ] . [8][1][ ][ ][ ] cm^3

5. In Chapter 5, you discovered the volume of $1,000 worth of nickels was the same as the volume of a cube with an edge length of 26 cm. Imagine wrapping this cube. What is the surface area of a cube filled with $1,000 worth of nickels?

Surface area ________________ cm^2

* 6. A cube has the same volume as $500 worth of nickels. Calculate the volume and surface area of this cube. Show your work.

6a. Volume of cube ________________ cm^3

The answer is not 2,197.

6b. Surface area of cube [2][ ][ ][ ] . [ ][ ][ ][ ] cm^2

       Maneuvers with Nickels and Numbers

Homework 6: How Much Wrapping Paper Do I Need?

1. Complete the following table. Fill in the missing units.

	Edge Length of Cube	Surface Area	Volume
1a.	5 cm		
1b.			216 cm^3
1c.			343 cm^3
1d.		384 cm^2	
1e.		486 cm^2	
1f. *Follow the pattern. What number is next?*			

2. Answer the following questions using the information in the table above.

2a. Is the volume of a cube always a larger number than the number for surface area? _________
Yes or No

2b. Which cube has a surface area that is larger than its volume? _________

2c. Which cube has a surface area and volume that are the same? _________

2d. When will the surface area of a cube be larger than the volume?

____

3. Some of the following statements are possible, while others are nonsense. Circle those that are possible.

a. Area = 450 cm

b. Volume = 450 cm^3

c. Length = 450 cm

d. Surface area = 13,450 cm^3

e. I bought enough paint to cover a 4,000 ft.^{2} wall.

f. There is 1,200 ft.^{2} of water in my pool.

g. Area = 450 cm^3

h. Volume = 317 ft.^{3}

j. Area = 317 miles

k. I bought enough paint to cover a 4,000 ft. wall.

m. There is 1,200 ft.^{3} of water in my swimming pool.

n. Under a microscope, I see an area of 1 mm^2.

4a. Build a cube using the pattern at the bottom of the page.

4b. Measure the edge length of the cube to the nearest 0.1 cm.

Edge length ________________ cm

4c. Calculate the volume of the cube.

Volume ________________ cm^3

4d. Calculate the surface area.

Surface area ________________ cm^2

- - - - - - - - - - - - - - - - - - - Cut below this line. -

Figure K

5. Look at the shading in the cube at the right. The three faces that are not showing are white.

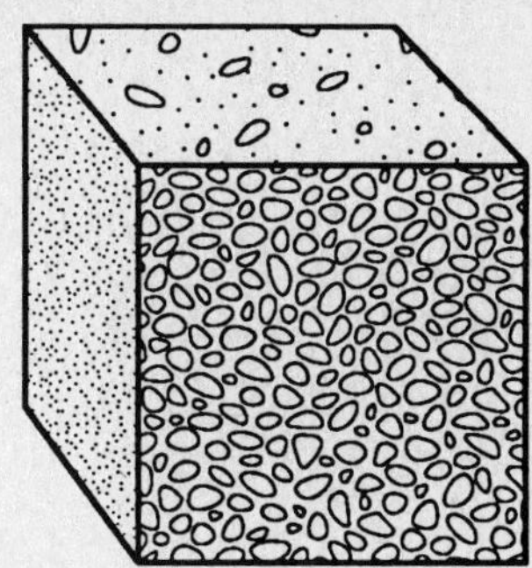

Figure L

5a. All of the patterns below will build a cube. However, some of them will not build the cube at the right. Predict which patterns will build this cube.

Predictions ______________________

5b. Cut out the patterns and build the cubes to check your predictions. Which patterns build this cube?

Answers ______________________

- Cut below this line. -

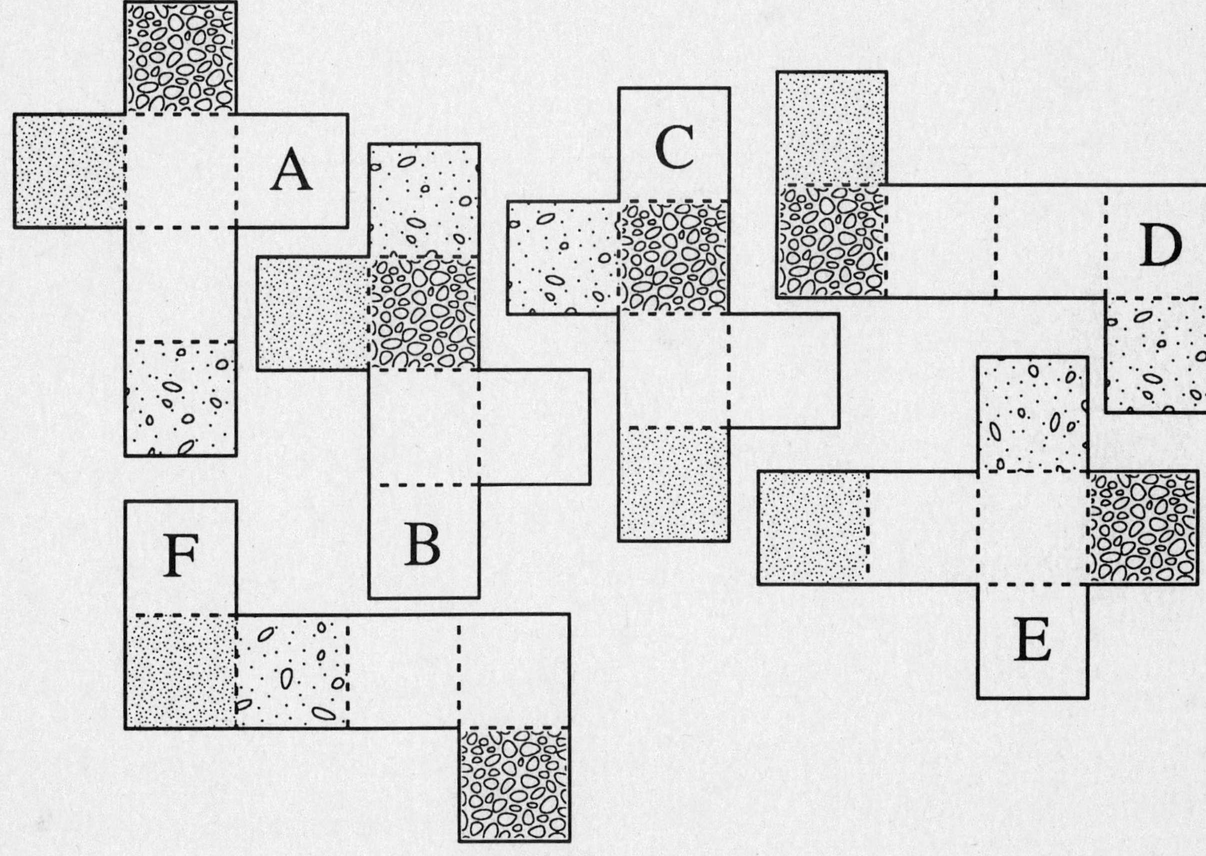

Figure M

7. How Many Faces Do You Count?

1. Three cubes are put together face-to-face to form a box.

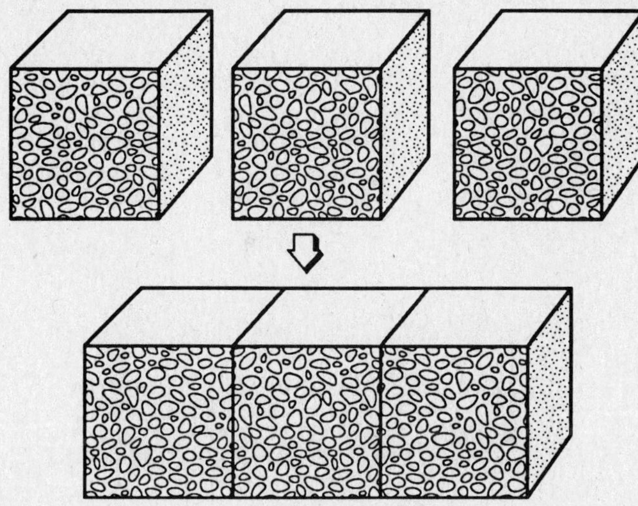

Figure A

Build Box A using Steps **a** through **c** and the pattern below.

a. Cut along the *dark* solid lines.
b. Fold the paper along the dashed lines.
c. Tape the sides together. (Save your box. You will need it later.)

- Cut below this line. -

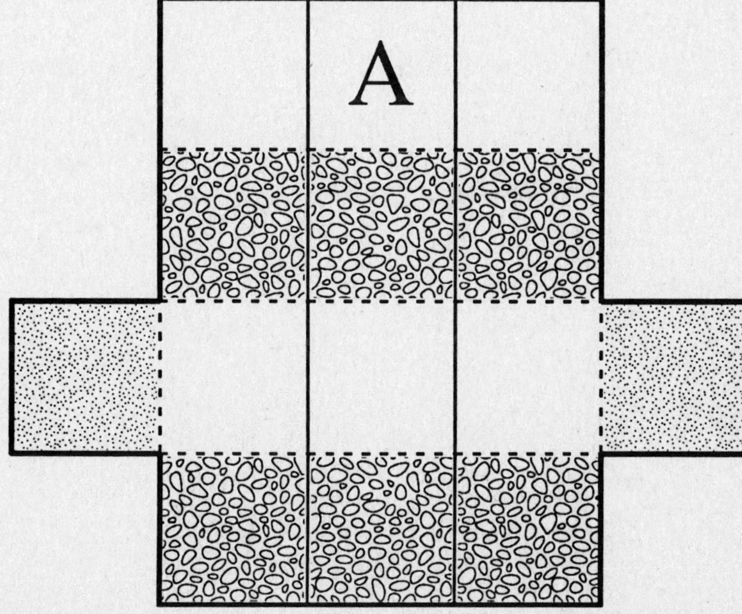

Figure B

Find your box's volume two different ways.

2. *First way:* Measure the dimensions of the box you built to the nearest cm.

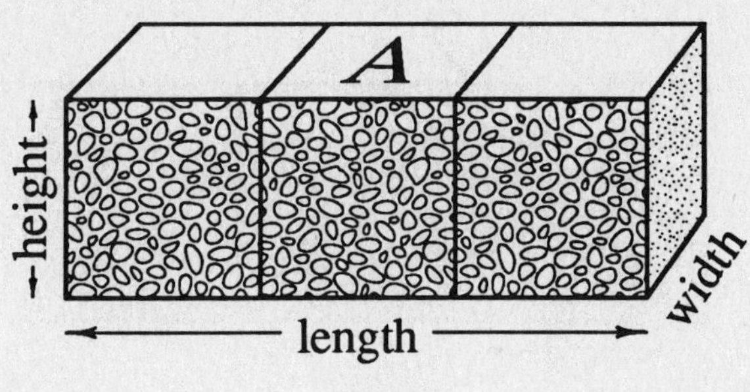

Figure C

2a. Length of box _______________ cm

2b. Width _______________

Put in units.

2c. Height _______________ cm

2d. Volume _______________

Put in units.

3. *Second way:* The box is built from three cubes. Find the volume of one cube.

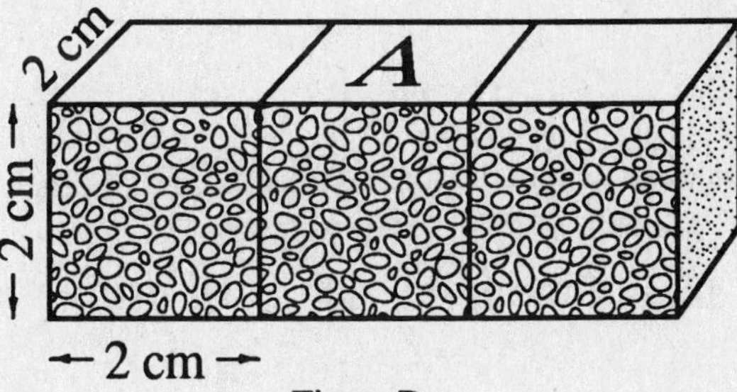

Figure D

3a. Volume of one cube _______________

Put in units.

3b. Volume of three cubes _______________ cm^3

Should agree with Problem 2d.

4. Which method do you like better? _____________________________________

Why? ____

5. If another cube was added to Figure D, what would the volume of the box be?

Volume of four cubes _______________ cm^3

6a. Three cubes are put together in the following sketch. Find the volume of the box using either method.

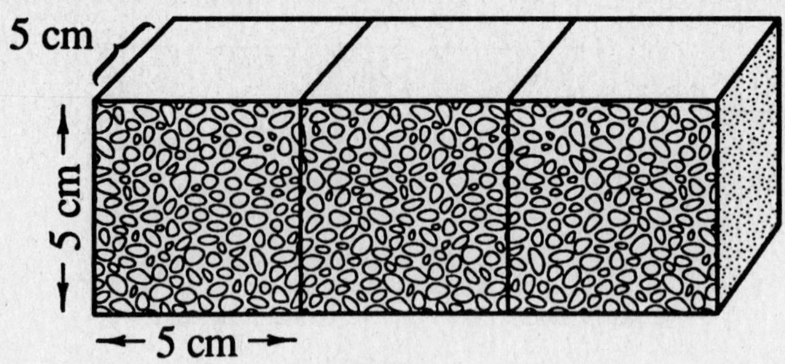

Figure E

Volume ______________________
Put in units.

6b. List the keystrokes you used for Problem 6a.

<table>
<tr><td>☐</td><td>☐</td><td>☐</td><td>☐</td><td>☐</td><td>☐</td></tr>
<tr><td>☐</td><td>☐</td><td>☐</td><td>☐</td><td>☐</td><td>☐</td></tr>
</table>

You may not need to use all the keystroke boxes.

7. Three cubes each having an edge length of 3.4482172 cm are put together to form a box. Calculate the volume of the box.

Volume ______________________ cm^3
You'll know.

8. Find the surface area of the following cube using the steps below.

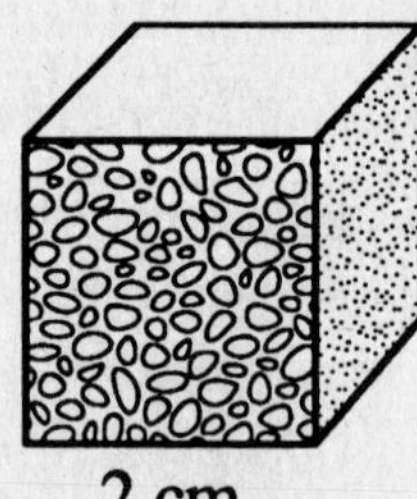

Figure F

8a. Number of faces ______________________

8b. Area of one face ______________________
Put in units.

8c. Surface area ______________________
Put in units.

Find the surface area of the box you built *two* different ways.

9. **First way:** Your box is built from three cubes. How many **square** faces make up the surface area of the box?

Figure G

9a. Answer _________________ square faces
The answer is not 18.

9b. Area of one square face _________________ cm^2

9c. Surface area of box _________________
Put in units.

10. **Second way:** The box you built has six faces. Not all the faces are the same shape. Notice there are two kinds of shapes.

Find the area of each face.

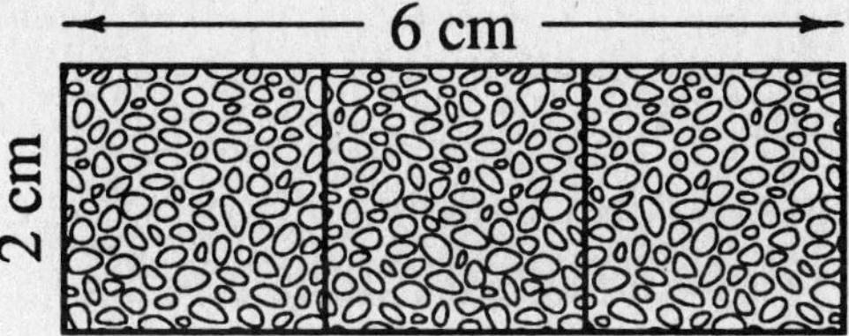

Figure H

10a. How many faces have the same shape as Figure H? _________________

10b. What is the area of one of these faces? _________________ cm^2

10c. What is the total area for this type of face? _________________
Put in units.

Second type of face:

Figure J

10d. How many faces have the same shape as Figure J? _________________

10e. What is the area of one of these faces? _________________ cm^2

10f. What is the total area for this type of face? _________________
Put in units.

10g. Surface area of box _________________ cm^2
Should agree with Problem 9c.

11a. Three cubes are put together in the following sketch. Find the surface area of the box using either method.

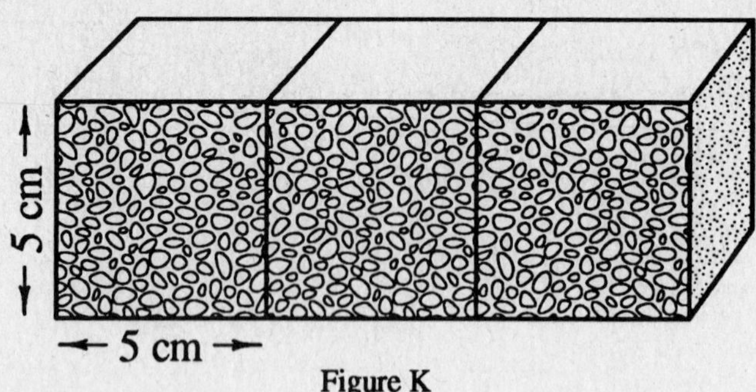

Surface area _________________ cm^2

11b. List the keystrokes you used for Problem 11a.

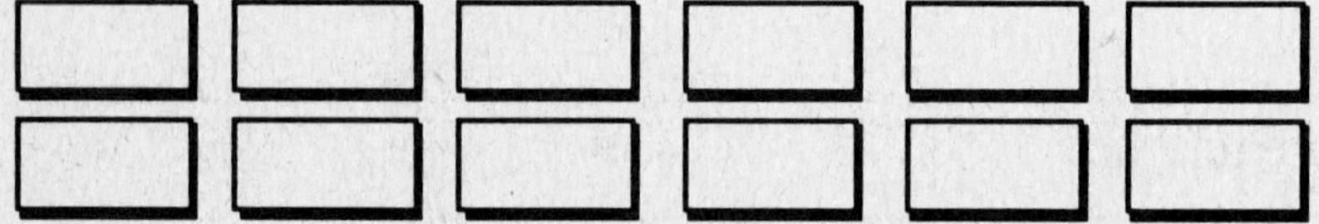

You may not need to use all the keystroke boxes.

12a. Three cubes are put together to form a box. The edge length of one of the cubes is 8.25 cm. Draw a sketch of this box.

12b. Calculate the volume of the box.

Volume $\boxed{\ \ \ \ \ \ \ \ 4\ .\ \ \ 4\ \ \ \ }$ cm^3

12c. Calculate the surface area of the box.

Surface area $\boxed{\ \ \ 5\ \ \ .\ \ \ \ \ 5\ }$ cm^2

13. The volume of the box in the following sketch is 1,029 cm^3. Calculate the edge length of one of the cubes using the steps below. Show your work.

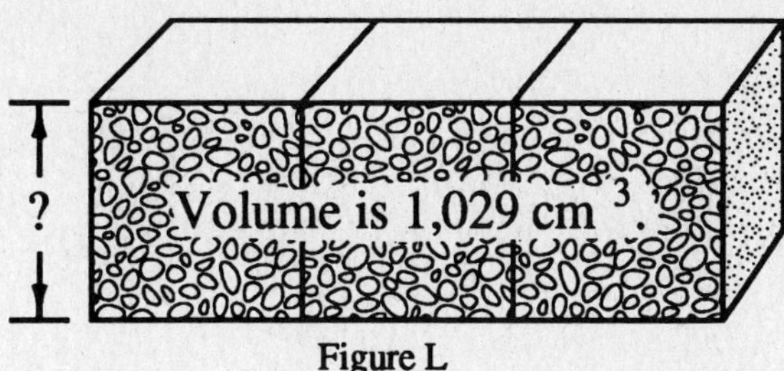

Figure L

13a. Volume of one cube _________________ cm^3

13b. Edge length of one cube _________________

Put in units.

14. Now that you know the edge length of one of the cubes, find the surface area of the whole box. Show your work.

Surface area _________________

Put in units.

15. Three cubes are put together in the following sketch. The volume of this box is 57.270266 cm^3. Calculate the surface area of the box. Show your work.

Figure M

15a. Edge length of one cube _________________ cm

Copy window.

15b. Surface area _________________ cm^2

You'll know.

 16. The surface area of the box in the sketch at the right is 504 cm^2. Calculate the edge length of one of the cubes using the following steps.

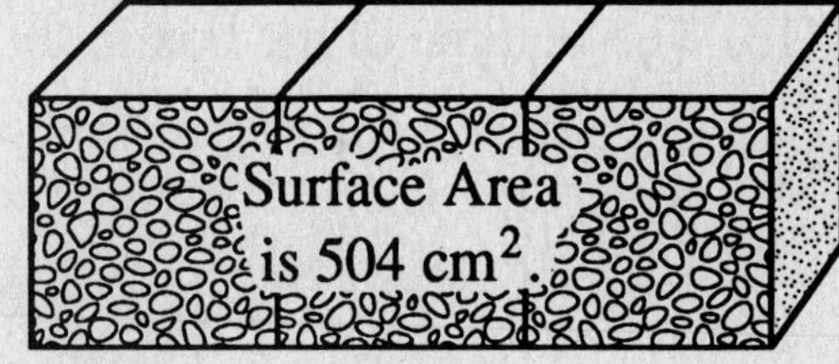

Figure N

16a. Number of square faces _________________

16b. Area of one face _________________ cm^2

16c. Edge length of cube _________________ cm

16d. Now that you know the edge length of one of the cubes, find the volume of the box.

Volume _________________ cm^3

17. The surface area of the box you built on page 87 is 56 cm^2. For practice, find the volume of the box using the following steps.

17a. Number of square faces _________________

17b. Area of one face _________________ cm^2

17c. Edge length of one cube _________________ cm

17d. Volume of one cube _________________ cm^3

17e. Volume of box _________________ cm^3

Should agree with
Problem 2d on page 89.

17f. If you do Problem 17 on the calculator, which keystrokes will you use?

56	÷				

18a. The surface area of a box built from three cubes is 1,400 cm^2. Draw a sketch of this box. Label its three dimensions.

18b. Calculate the volume of this box. Show your work.

Volume _________________ cm^3

Try It Out!

1. Build Box B using the pattern below.

2. Is Box B smaller or larger than Box A from page 87?

   Answer ________________
   Smaller or Larger

3. Measure the dimensions of Box B to the nearest 0.1 cm.

3a. Length ________________ cm

3b. Width ________________
   Put in units.

3c. Height ________________
   Put in units.

4. Calculate the volume of Box B. ________________ cm^3

5. Calculate the surface area of Box B. ________________
   Put in units.

- Cut below this line. -

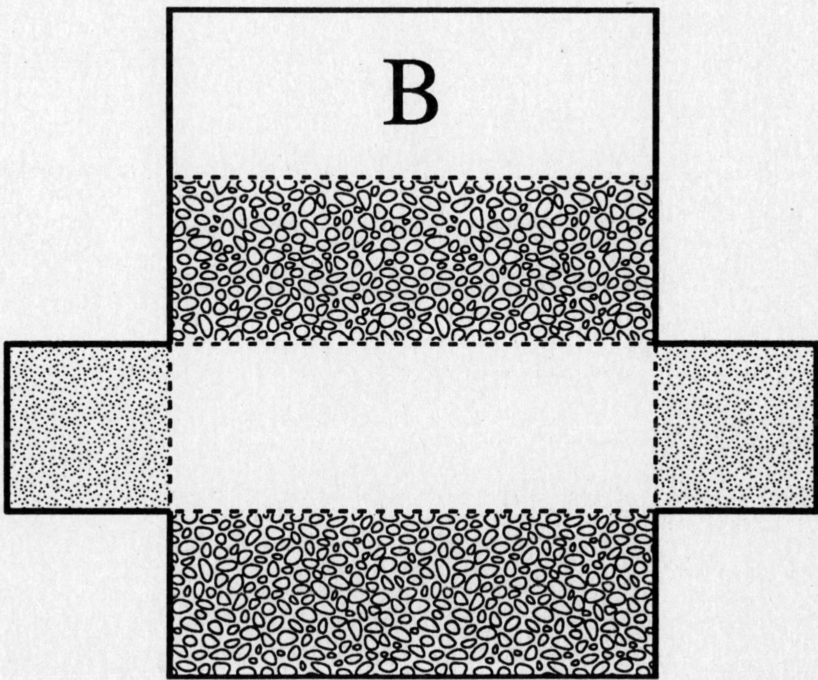

Figure P

6a. The sketch at the right is built from four cubes.
Find the volume of the stack.

Volume _________________ cm^3
You'll know.

6b. List your keystrokes.

| 6.2996053 | | | |

| | | |

6c. Find the surface area of the stack.

Surface area [ ][ ][ ].[*3*][*3*][ ][ ][ ] cm^2

6.2996053 cm

Figure Q

---

7. Cubes are put together face-to-face in a row to form boxes.
Complete the following table. The first one is done for you.

	Number of Cubes	Square Faces on Box	Sketch
7a.	2	10	
7b.	3		
7c.	4		
7d.	5		

✱ **8.** One hundred cubes are put together face-to-face to form a box.
How many square faces does the box have?

Answer _________________ faces

                    Maneuvers with Nickels and Numbers

9. Put Box A next to another Box A to make the following box. Measure the dimensions of the box to the nearest cm.

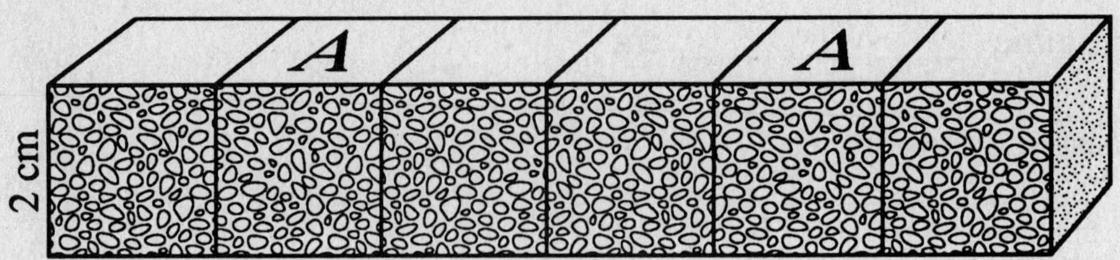

Figure R

9a. What is the volume? _________________
Put in units.

9b. What is the surface area? _________________ cm^2
The answer is less than 112 cm^2.

10. Put Box A on top of another Box A to build the following box.

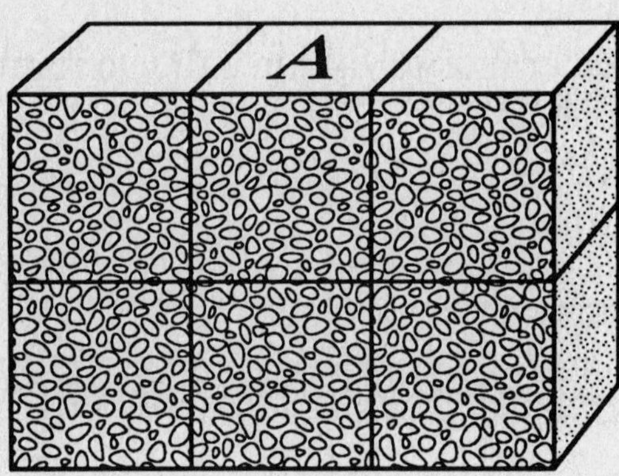

Figure S

10a. What is the volume? _________________
Put in units.

10b. What is the surface area? _________________
Put in units.

11. Why are the volumes the same in Problems 9a and 10a?

____

12. Why is the surface area smaller in Problem 10b?

____

13a. Work with three classmates. Build a figure using four of the boxes labeled "A." Remember, the boxes must be put together face-to-face.

13b. Draw a sketch of your figure.

13c. Calculate the volume and surface area of your figure.

Volume ________________
Put in units.

Surface area ________________
Put in units.

13d. Draw a sketch of the figure that has the largest possible surface area. Remember, the boxes must be put together face-to-face. Find the surface area of your sketch.

Largest surface area ________________ cm^2

13e. Draw a sketch of the figure that has the smallest possible surface area. Find the surface area of your sketch.

Smallest surface area ________________ cm^2

Homework 7: How Many Faces Do You Count?

1. Five cubes are put together in the following sketch.
   The volume of the box is 625 cm^3. Calculate the surface area of the box using the steps below.

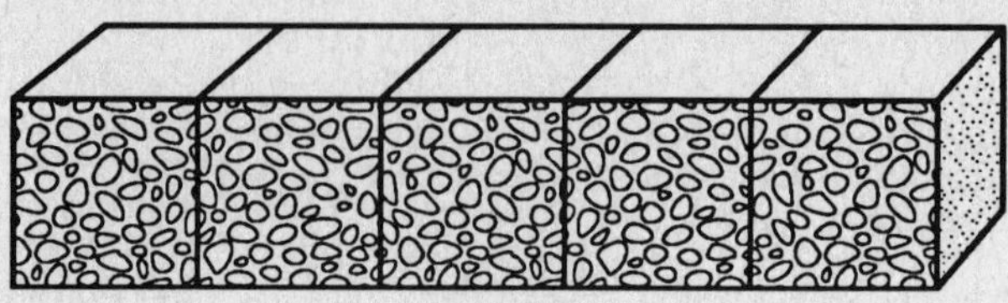

Figure T

1a. Volume of one cube _________________ cm^3

1b. Edge length of cube _________________
   Put in units.

1c. Area of one face _________________ cm^2

1d. Number of faces _________________

1e. Surface area of box _________________
   Put in units.

2. Five congruent cubes are joined to form a box similar to Figure T.
   The volume of this box is 635 cm^3. Find the surface area of the box.

Surface area $\boxed{\ \ |\ \ |\ 5\ |.|\ 5\ |\ \ |\ \ |\ \ }$ cm^2

3. Four cubes are put together in the following sketch.
   The volume of the sketch is 17,752.373 cm^3. Calculate the surface area.
   Show your work.

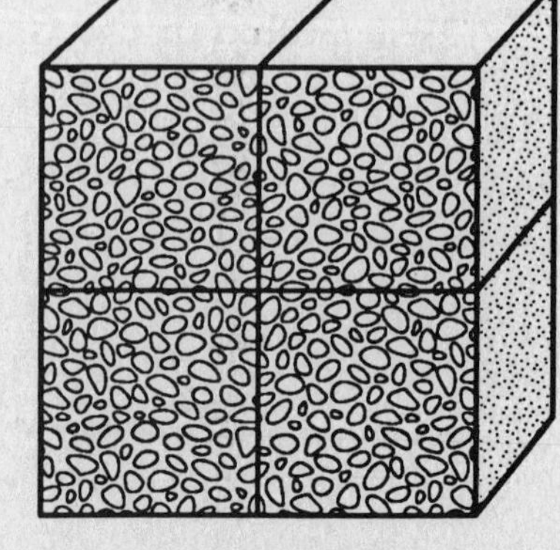

Figure U

Surface area _________________ cm^2
   You'll know.

4. Six cubes are joined face-to-face to form the following sketch. The surface area of the sketch is 150 cm^2. Find its volume using the steps below.

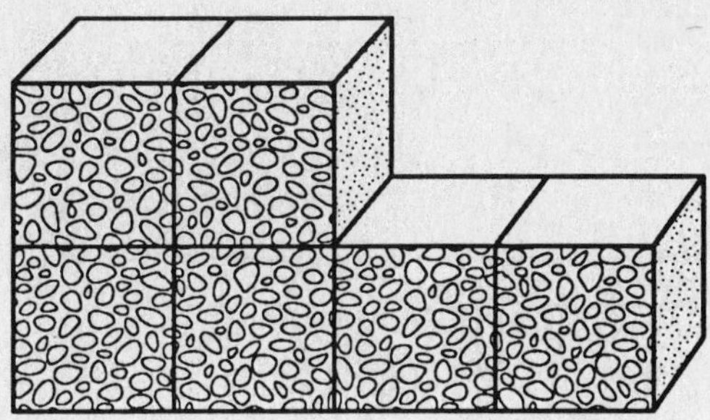

Figure V

4a. Number of square faces _________________

4b. Area of one square face _________________ cm^2

4c. Edge length of cube _________________ cm

4d. Volume of figure _________________ cm^3

5. Six cubes are joined face-to-face to form the following sketch. The surface area of the sketch is 160 cm^2.

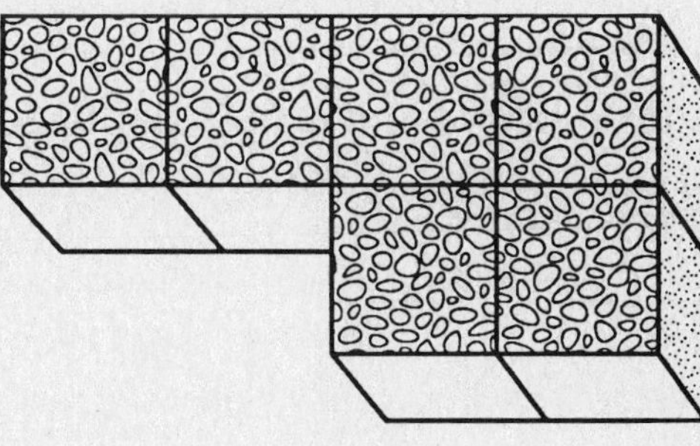

Figure W

5a. What can you predict about the volume of this sketch? Hint: Look at Problem 4.

____

5b. Calculate the volume of Figure W. Show your work.

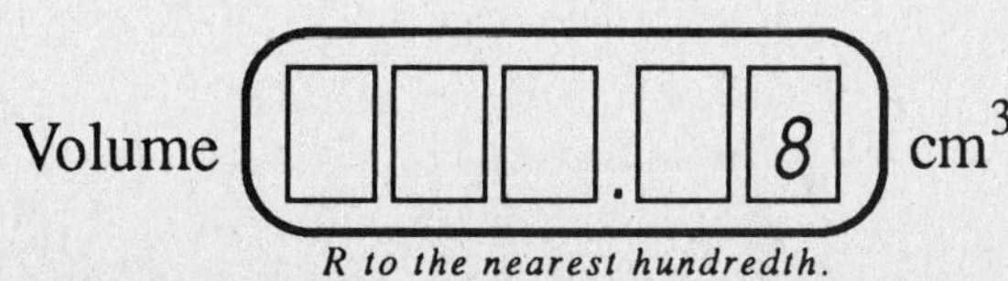

R to the nearest hundredth.

6. The following sketch is built from three congruent cubes.
   Find the volume of the sketch.

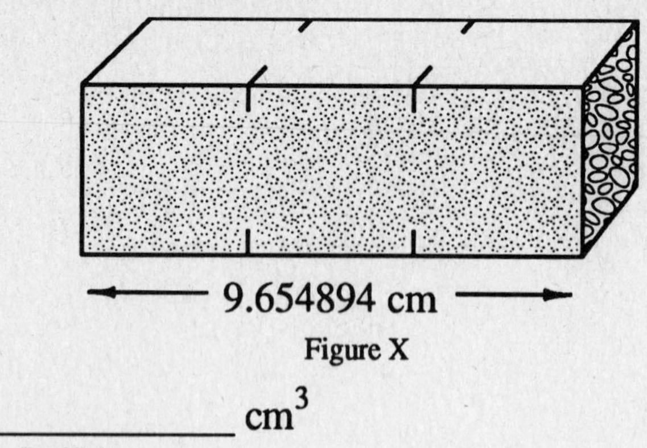

◄——— 9.654894 cm ———►

Figure X

Volume ________________ cm^3

You'll know.

7a. The cube at the right is a sketch.
    Calculate its volume using $\boxed{y^x}$.

Volume $\boxed{}\,\boxed{}\,\boxed{8}.\boxed{}\,\boxed{2}\,\boxed{}$ cm^3

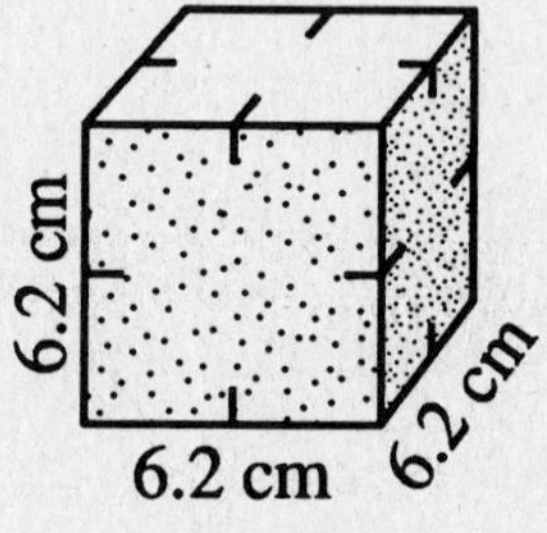

7b. List your keystrokes for Problem 7a.

$\boxed{}\;\boxed{}\;\boxed{}\;\boxed{}$

7c. Eight smaller, identical cubes are put together to form the cube in
    Figure Y. What are the dimensions of one of the smaller cubes?

Dimensions __________ cm, __________ cm, __________ cm
          Length   *Width*   *Height*

7d. Find the volume of one of the smaller cubes using the $\boxed{y^x}$ key.

Volume $\boxed{}\,\boxed{}.\boxed{7}\,\boxed{}\,\boxed{}$ cm^3

7e. List your keystrokes.

$\boxed{6.2}\;\boxed{}\;\boxed{}\;\boxed{}\;\boxed{}\;\boxed{}\;\boxed{}$

7f. How can you use your answer from Problem 7d to find the volume of the
    cube in Figure Y?

____

____

8a. Five congruent cubes form the sketch at the right. Calculate the volume of the sketch.

Volume _______________ cm^3
You'll know.

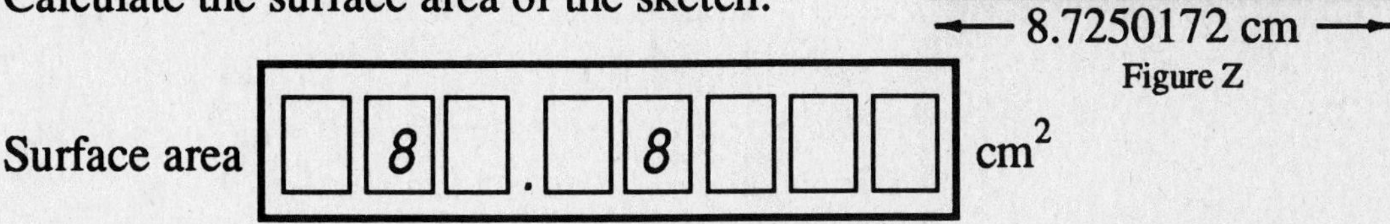

8.7250172 cm

Figure Z

8b. Calculate the surface area of the sketch.

Surface area | | 8 | | . | | 8 | | | | cm^2

9. Nine cubes form the sketch at the right. Notice that the sketch is not a cube.

9a. What is the volume? _______________
Put in units.

9b. What is the surface area?

Surface area _______________
Put in units.

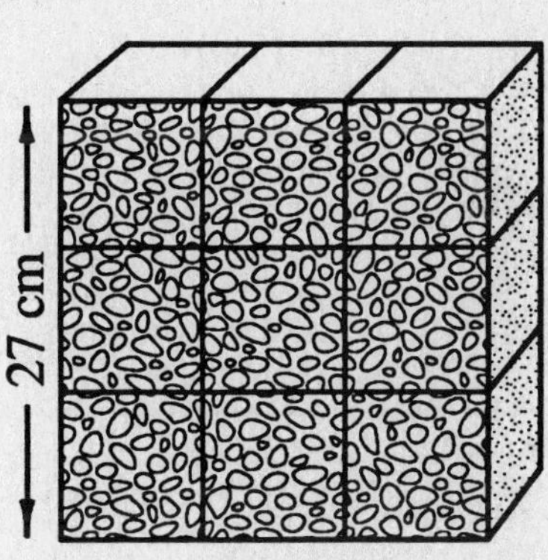

27 cm

Figure AA

10. The cube in the middle is taken away.

10a. What is the new volume?

Volume _______________ cm^3

10b. What is the new surface area?

Surface area _______________
Put in units.

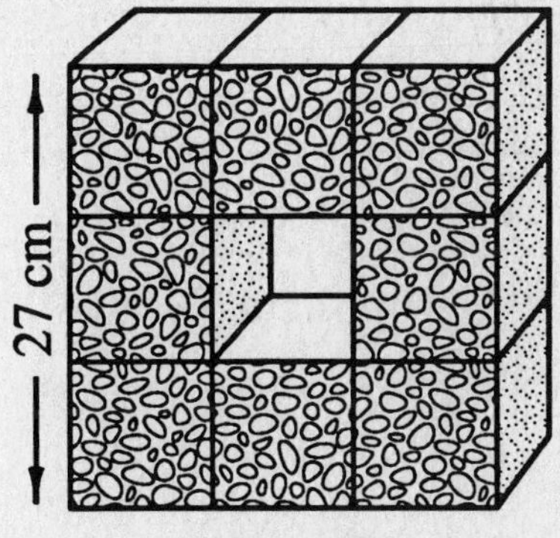

27 cm

Figure BB

11. Compare Problems 9 and 10.

11a. Did the volume increase or decrease? _______________

Why? ____

11b. Did the surface area increase or decrease? _______________

Why? ____

12. Complete the following table. The figures in the following table are built from centimeter cubes. Remember to put in the units.

	Figure	Volume	Surface Area
12a.			
12b.			
12c.			
12d.		7 cm^3	30 cm^2
12e.	*You make one up.*		

8. How Big Is It?

British Gold Heist Nets Record $37,500,000

1. According to newspaper accounts, $37,500,000 in gold was stolen from a Brinks warehouse in London, England, on November 26, 1983. You be the detective and calculate the weight of all this gold.

1a. On Monday, November 28, 1983, gold cost $393.25 for every troy ounce. How many troy ounces were stolen?

Answer   [ ] [ ] [*3*] [ ] [ ] .   troy ounces

Round to the nearest troy ounce.
Incidentally, the answer is a palindrome.

> Gold is not weighed in "everyday" ounces. It is measured in ***troy ounces***. There are 12 troy ounces in a pound.

1b. Calculate how many pounds were stolen.

Answer   [ ] [ ] [*4*] [ ] .   pounds

Round to the nearest pound.

2a. Convert the number of pounds that were stolen to kilograms.

Remember, 1 kg = 2.2 lbs.

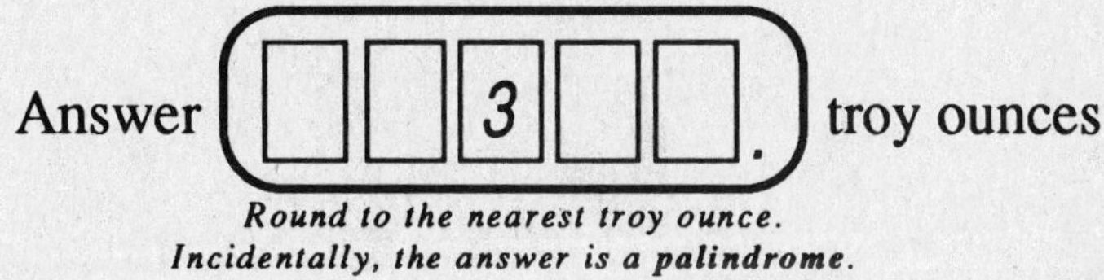

Weight _______________ lbs. = [ ] [ ] [*1*] [*2*] . [ ] [ ] [ ] [ ]   kg

Copy answer from
Problem 1b.

2b. Convert your answer to grams. 1 kg = 1,000 g

Weight of gold   [ ] [*6*] [ ] [ ] [ ] [ ] [ ] .   g

R to the nearest gram.

3. According to the newspaper, 76 gold bars were stolen. How many pounds did each bar weigh?

Answer 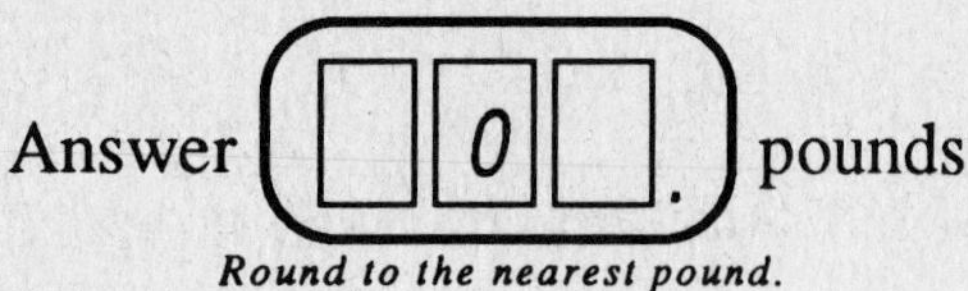 pounds

Round to the nearest pound.

4. Circle the character who is lifting a reasonable number of the stolen gold bars in the cartoon.

5. Look in the business section of a major newspaper to find the price of gold yesterday. The paper lists the price of one troy ounce of gold.

5a. Yesterday's date _______________

5b. Price of gold $_______________ per troy ounce

5c. How much would the stolen gold be worth now? Show your work.

     Answer $_______________

5d. Is the stolen gold worth more now? _______________

Yes or No

How Much Does Gold Weigh?

1 cubic centimeter of gold
weighs 19.3 grams.

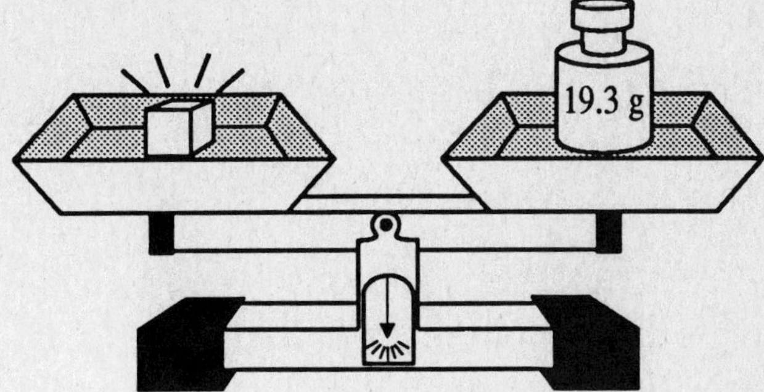

2 cm^3 of gold weigh 38.6 grams.

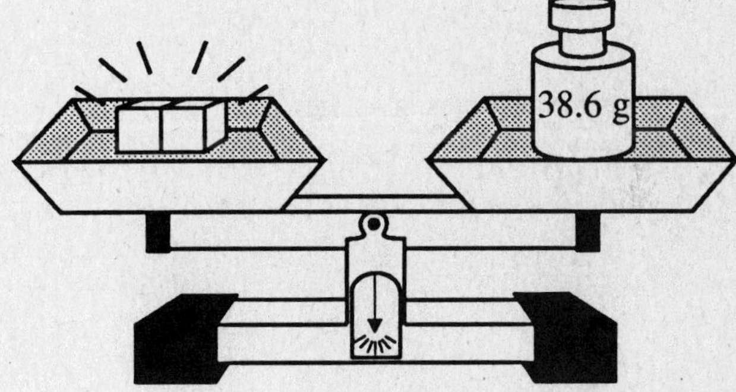

If you know the volume (the number of cm^3) of gold, you can calculate the total weight.

1. Find the weight of 6 cm^3
   of gold.

   Weight _______________ g

2. Find the weight of 13 cm^3 of gold.

   Weight _______________ g

If you know the total weight, you can calculate the volume of gold.

19.3 g of gold has a volume
of 1 cubic centimeter.

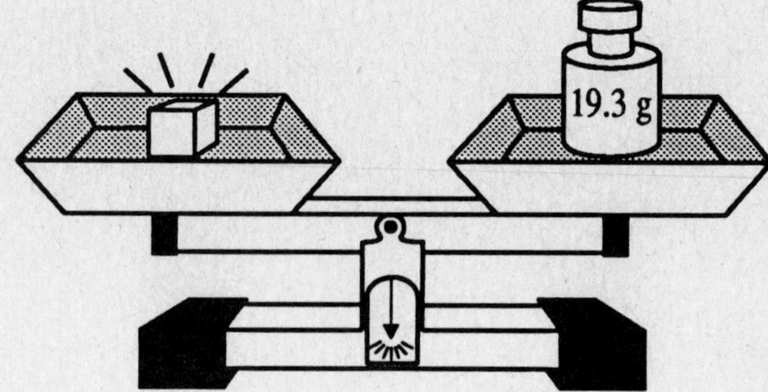

77.2 g of gold has a volume
of 4 cm^3.

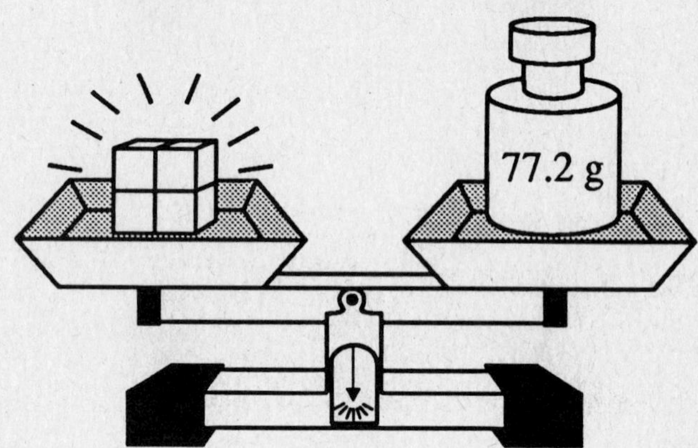

3a. Find how many cm^3 weigh 386 g.

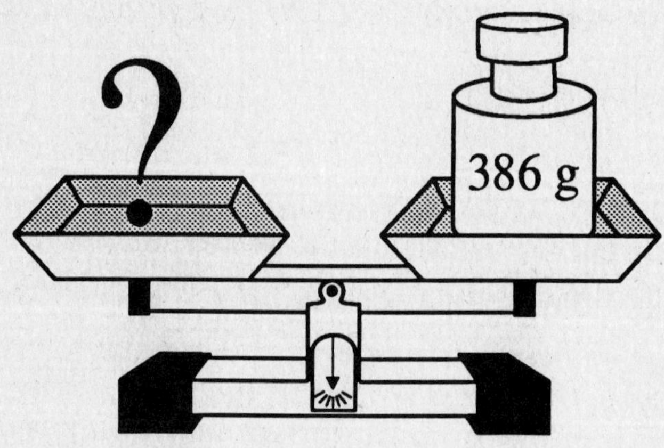

Volume _________________ cm^3

3b. List your keystrokes for Problem 3a.

4. Find the volume of 3,860 grams of gold.

Volume _________________ cm^3

Where Could the Stolen Gold Be Hidden?

1. Be the detective and predict where the thieves hid the gold. ____________

2. You know the weight of the stolen gold in grams. Use this information to calculate the volume of the stolen gold in cm^3.

____________ g of gold has a volume of

. cm^3.

Copy answer from Problem 2b on page 105.

R to the nearest cubic cm.

3. If this gold was melted and made into the shape of one big cube, what would the edge length of the cube be?

Edge length _________________ cm

R to the nearest cm.

4. The thieves hid the stolen bars in the attic closet, under the trapdoor in the basement, or in the freezer in the garage.

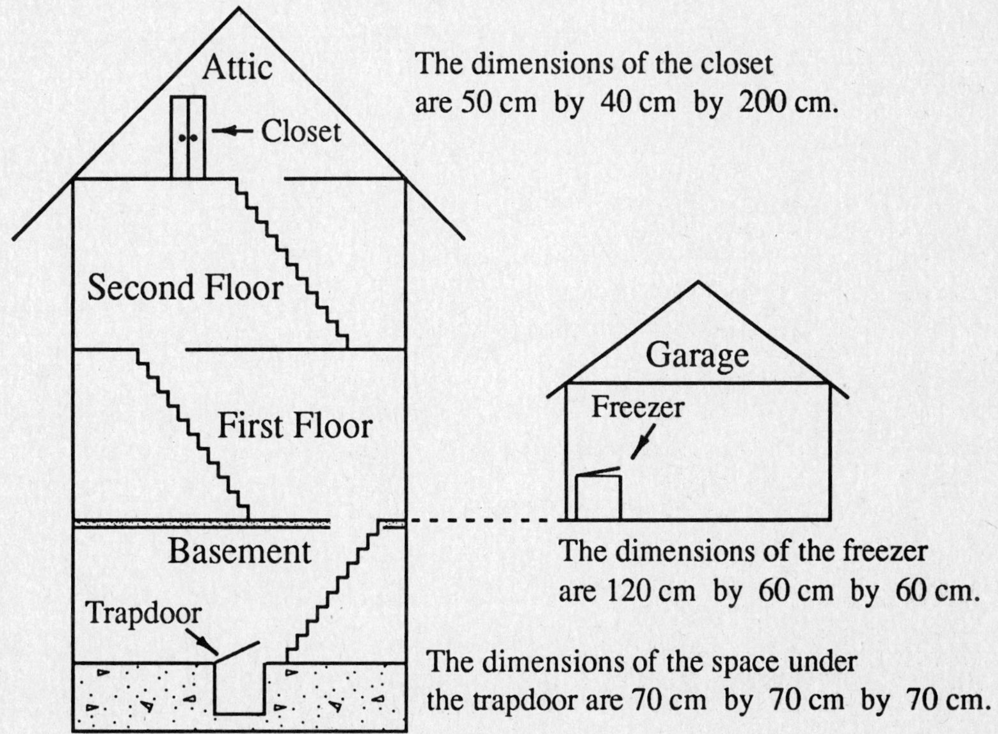

4a. In which places would the gold fit? _________________________________

4b. In which place do you think the thieves hid the gold? _______________

Why? ____

How Much Gold Could You Carry?

1. Circle the student carrying a reasonable amount of gold in the following picture. Notice the edge lengths of the cubes are labeled under each student.

2. Predict the *volume* of gold you could carry. Hint: 1 cm^3 of gold weighs 19.3 g.

    Answer _________________ cm^3

3. Calculate the volume of gold you could carry using the following steps.

3a. How many pounds can you carry for a block? _________________ lbs.

3b. Convert your answer from Problem 3a to grams. Show your work.

    Answer _________________ g
    R to the nearest g.

3c. How many cm^3 of gold can you carry? Remember one cubic centimeter of gold weighs 19.3 grams. Show your work.

    Answer _________________ cm^3
    R to the nearest cubic cm.

    Compare your answer for Problem 3c with your prediction in Problem 2.

3d. Imagine this gold was melted and made into the shape of a cube. What would the edge length of this cube be?

    Edge length _________________ cm
    R to the nearest cm.
    Compare with Problem 1.

Does It Stack Up?

Mr. Peabody works in the Flower Your Fancy Flower Shop. He stacks flower pots, one inside the other, as shown below. The total height of one pot is 13 cm. Its rim is 4 cm.

1. How tall is a stack of three flower pots?

   Answer _________________
   Put in units.

2. How tall is a stack of five flower pots?

   Answer _________________
   Put in units.

3. How tall is a stack of fifty flower pots?

   Answer _________________
   Put in units.

4. A stack of flower pots is 157 cm tall. How many flower pots are in the stack? Show your work.

   Answer _________________ flower pots

5. Mr. Peabody stores these pots underneath a shelf that is 100 cm (1 meter) from the ground. How many pots can he fit in one stack underneath the shelf? Show your work.

   Answer _________________ flower pots

Who Would Ever See $10,000 in Quarters?

You need 5 quarters to run the machines at the Silver Coin Laundromat. The following graph shows how much money was collected from the machines each day for one week. Use the graph to answer the questions below.

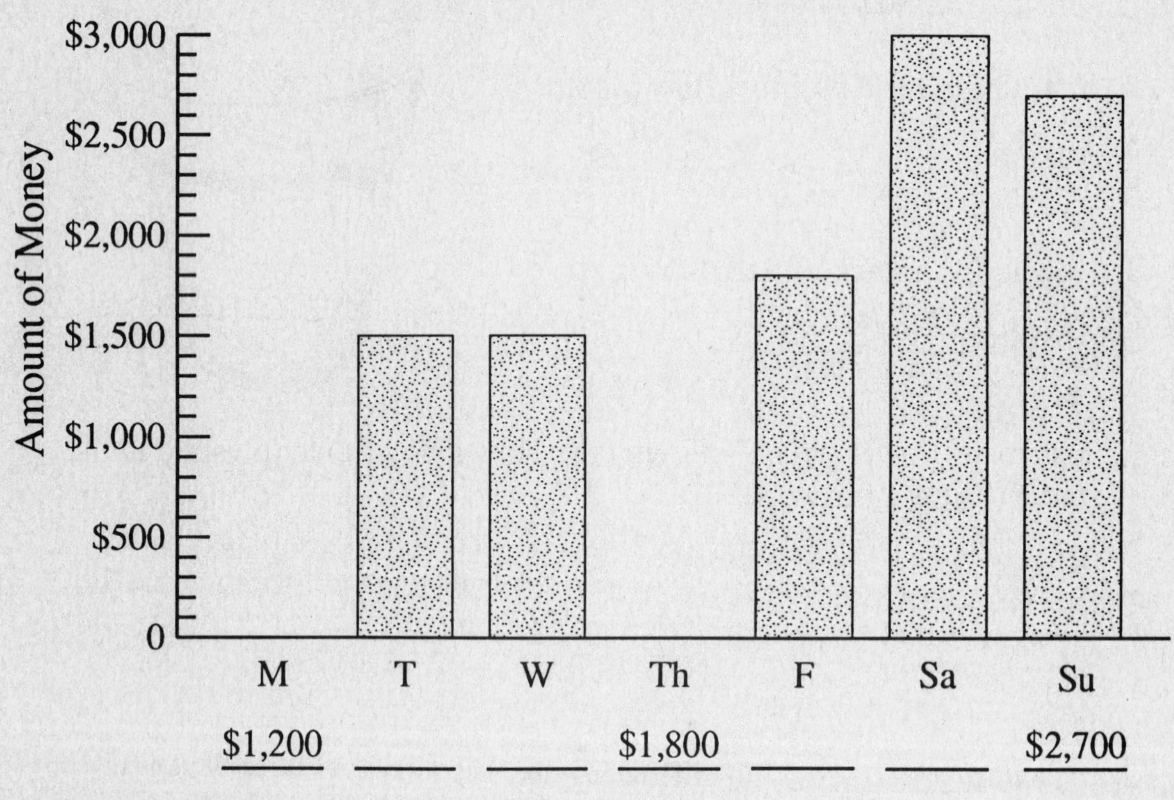

1. Draw the bars for Monday and Thursday.

2. Write the amount collected on Tuesday, Wednesday, Friday, and Saturday under each bar.

3. How much money did the laundromat collect for this week?

   Answer $________________

4. How many quarters did the laundromat collect for the week?

   Answer ________________ quarters

   The answer is not 3,375.

5. If one quarter weighs 5.67 grams, how many *pounds* do a week's worth of quarters weigh? Show your work.

Weight of quarters _________________ lbs.

Round to nearest pound.

6. The owner, Mr Suds, is able to carry 50 pounds. Would Mr. Suds be able to carry a week's worth of quarters to the bank?

Answer _________________

Yes or No

7a. Would Mr. Suds be able to carry just the quarters collected on Monday?

Answer _________________

Yes or No

7b. Why or why not? Show your work.

✶ 8. If each machine ran 16 loads on Monday, calculate the number of machines in the Silver Coin Laundromat. Remember, you need 5 quarters to run one load for each machine.

Answer _________________ machines

How Thick Is This Piece of Paper?

Paper comes in packages called "reams."
Each ream of paper contains 500 sheets.

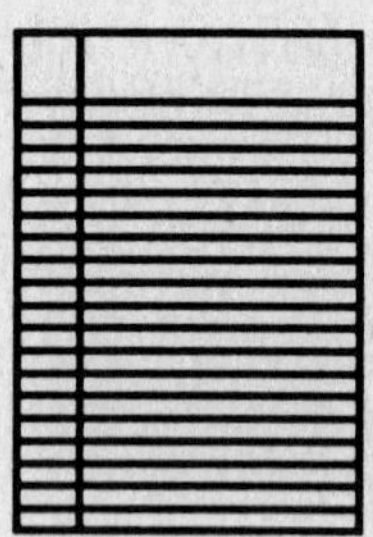

 1. A ream of paper is 5 cm thick.
What is the thickness of one piece of paper?

1a. Thickness ________________ cm

1b. Change your answer to inches. 1 in. = 2.54 cm

Thickness | 0 | . | | | 3 | | | in.

Notice the unit.

2. What is the area of a piece of $8\frac{1}{2}$ in. by 11 in. paper?

Area ______________ in.^{2}

✱ 3a. What is the surface area of this same piece of paper?
Hint: The paper has six faces. Four of them are *very*
small! Show your work.

Surface area | | | 7 | . | 1 | | | | in.^{2}

3b. Round your answer to the nearest tenth.

Surface area (| | 7 | . |) in.^{2}

Does Tile Floor You?

Jackie is going to tile her kitchen floor.
She measures the dimensions of her kitchen
floor. The length is 12.5 feet and the width
is 6.5 feet. She will have to cut some of the
tiles near the edge so they will fit.

1. Each tile is 1 square foot. How many *whole* tiles does Jackie need?

   Answer _______________ tiles

2. Twelve of these tiles come in a box. How many whole boxes should
   Jackie buy?

   Answer _______________ boxes

3. If each box costs $23.88, how much will Jackie's order cost?

   Answer $_______________

4. How many square-inch tiles are needed to tile Jackie's kitchen floor?
   12 in. = 1 ft.

   Answer _______________
          Put in units.

5. If 720 square-inch tiles come in a box, how many whole boxes are
   needed?

   Answer _______________
          Put in units.

6. How much would it cost to tile Jackie's kitchen floor with square-inch
   tiles? Each box costs $14.40.

   Answer $_______________

7. Which order would be more expensive? _______________

   How much more? $_______________

                              Maneuvers with Nickels and Numbers

How Big Is Your Classroom?

1. Measure the dimensions of your classroom to the nearest inch. Draw a sketch of your classroom and include the dimensions on the grid.

2. Cut out an advertisement for square tile from your local newspaper. Make sure the advertisement lists the cost and the size of the tile.

3. What is the size of the tile in the advertisement? _________________

   Put in units.

4. What is the cost of the tile in the advertisement? _________________

   Put in units.

5. How much would it cost to tile your classroom floor using the tile in the advertisement? Show your work.

   Answer $_________________